NEW DIRECTIONS FOR COMMUNITY COLLEGES

Arthur M. Cohen
EDITOR-IN-CHIEF

Florence B. Brawer
ASSOCIATE EDITOR

Paula Zeszotarski
PUBLICATION COORDINATOR

Transfer Students: Trends and Issues

Frankie Santos Laanan
University of Illinois at Urbana-Champaign

EDITOR

Number 114, Summer 2001

JOSSEY-BASS
San Francisco

ERIC®

Clearinghouse for Community Colleges

TRANSFER STUDENTS: TRENDS AND ISSUES
Frankie Santos Laanan (ed.)
New Directions for Community Colleges, no. 114
Volume XXX, number 2
Arthur M. Cohen, Editor-in-Chief
Florence B. Brawer, Associate Editor

New Directions for Community Colleges is indexed in Current Index to Journals in Education (ERIC).

Microfilm copies of issues and articles are available in 16mm and 35mm, as well as microfiche in 105mm, through University Microfilms Inc., 300 North Zeeb Road, Ann Arbor, Michigan 48106-1346.

ISSN 0194-3081   ISBN 0-7879-5779-8

NEW DIRECTIONS FOR COMMUNITY COLLEGES is part of The Jossey-Bass Higher and Adult Education Series and is published quarterly by Jossey-Bass Inc., 350 Sansome Street, San Francisco, California 94104-1342, in association with the ERIC Clearinghouse for Community Colleges. Periodicals postage paid at San Francisco, California, and at additional mailing offices. POSTMASTER: Send address changes to New Directions for Community Colleges, Jossey-Bass Inc., 350 Sansome Street, San Francisco, California 94104-1342.

SUBSCRIPTIONS cost $63.00 for individuals and $115.00 for institutions, agencies, and libraries. Prices subject to change.

THE MATERIAL in this publication is based on work sponsored wholly or in part by the Office of Educational Research and Improvement, U.S. Department of Education, under contract number ED-99-CO-0010. Its contents do not necessarily reflect the views of the Department or any other agency of the U.S. Government.

EDITORIAL CORRESPONDENCE should be sent to the Editor-in-Chief, Arthur M. Cohen, at the ERIC Clearinghouse for Community Colleges, University of California, 3051 Moore Hall, Box 951521, Los Angeles, California 90095-1521. All manuscripts receive anonymous reviews by external referees.

Cover photograph © Rene Sheret, After Image, Los Angeles, California, 1990.

Printed in the United States of America on acid-free recycled paper containing 100 percent recovered waste paper, of which at least 20 percent is postconsumer waste.

CONTENTS

EDITOR'S NOTES

Transfer has been a central mission in America's community colleges (Cohen and Brawer, 1996), but they emphasize it to varying degrees. Community colleges are in a strategic position to increase students' access to and participation in the transfer pipeline. At the community college, different curricula provide academic preparation for students seeking to transfer to a four-year college or university. In addition, academic services, such as transfer centers, have been created to facilitate students' progress toward their transfer goal. Additionally, academic programs, such as honors or scholars programs, provide students with rigorous academic training as well as with opportunities to participate in formal articulation agreements with senior institutions. Although institutional support may be provided by two- and four-year colleges, students still face numerous challenges upon transferring. Furthermore, the extent to which students are successful academically, socially, and personally has been an important policy question for community colleges. In the wake of accountability mandates, institutions of higher learning are committed to understanding the success of transfer students in terms of their prior academic preparation at the two-year institution as well as their ultimate experience at the senior institution.

For students to succeed at senior institutions, institutional leaders at community colleges need to assess and evaluate various student outcomes. Reliable and valid research designs will inform administrators, faculty members, student affairs professionals, and personnel at two-year institutions about the extent to which they are providing academic training and support services for transfer students. Community college leaders must reflect on lessons learned and begin charting their mission to address the changing demographics of students.

This volume builds on previous issues of *New Directions for Community Colleges* edited by Cohen (1994) and Rifkin (1996), and it attempts to address the critical issues facing students moving through the educational pipeline. The objective of this volume is to evaluate recent research and policy discussions about transfer students. Specifically, the chapters address three broad themes: research, student and academic issues, and institutional factors. These chapters are important for various audiences, including community college administrators, faculty members, student affairs professionals, researchers, and students. Furthermore, they inform policymakers as well as four-year institutions about issues affecting transfer students.

In Chapter One, I present a synthesis of the research literature on transfer students by highlighting information about transfer behavior, the transfer adjustment process, and several perspectives on college adjustment. In Chapter Two, Eboni M. Zamani examines programs to facilitate transfer in community colleges and highlights common program elements and recommendations for systematically enhancing student transfer to four-year institutions. In Chapter Three, Herald R. Kane describes the history of honors programs in California and identifies pivotal contributions of intersegmental transfer agreements at community colleges. He concludes the chapter with implications for college students and faculty members. Wynetta Y. Lee, in Chapter Four, discusses an important population enrolled in community colleges—minority students—and examines issues for minority students in higher education. Specifically, Lee addresses issues of college transfer from the perspective of policy, programs, performance assessment, and constituents. In Chapter Five, James C. Arnold highlights findings from a recent study of students who transfer between community colleges and public universities in the state of Oregon.

In Chapter Six, Carol A. Kozeracki examines the role of research in studying transfer students and presents a variety of model studies for the effective assessment of the transfer process. In Chapter Seven, Brenda Johnson-Benson, Peter B. Geltner, and Steven K. Steinberg describe the motivating factors that led to the research and collaborative efforts to uncover issues pertaining to transfer students at one community college in Southern California. The authors discuss the evolution of the research study and the policy implications relevant to institutional research, faculty, student affairs, and other aspects of the college environment. In Chapter Eight, Latrice E. Eggleston and I discuss post-transfer support services at four-year institutions and present strategies that may help administrators and faculty members assist this growing population. Finally, in Chapter Nine, two community college leaders address the implementation of innovative approaches to transfer. Phoebe K. Helm shares her expertise on the role and function of a community college president and the extent to which an executive officer of a college can facilitate and foster the preparation of transfer students. Arthur M. Cohen describes institutional strategies to incorporate new approaches to transfer.

To solve the transfer puzzle, both two- and four-year institutions must work in synergy to address the needs of students who aspire to transfer to a four-year institution. These chapters provide valuable information that speaks to various constituencies—administrators, faculty members, student affairs professionals, and other college personnel—all of whom are equally important in facilitating and fostering the successful preparation and transition of transfer students.

Frankie Santos Laanan
Editor

References

Cohen, A. M. (ed.). *Relating Curriculum and Transfer*. New Directions for Community Colleges, no. 86. San Francisco: Jossey-Bass, 1994.

Cohen, A. M., and Brawer, F. B. *Policies and Programs That Affect Transfer*. Washington, D.C.: American Council on Education, 1996.

Rifkin, T. (ed.). *Transfer and Articulation: Improving Policies to Meet New Needs*. New Directions for Community Colleges, no. 96. San Francisco: Jossey-Bass, 1996.

FRANKIE SANTOS LAANAN is assistant professor of community college leadership in the Department of Human Resource Education at the University of Illinois at Urbana-Champaign. His research interests include community colleges, transfer and articulation, and college student development.

1

This chapter discusses the trends surrounding transfer students and highlights issues affecting these students. Also presented is a synthesis of research on transfer students, post-transfer adjustment process, and perspectives on college adjustment.

Transfer Student Adjustment

Frankie Santos Laanan

Over eleven hundred campuses strong, American community colleges enroll almost half of the nation's undergraduates each fall and half of all first-time freshmen, offering them a diverse and flexible curriculum that meets their academic and vocational goals (Cohen and Brawer, 1996). Public and independent community colleges are found in every state. According to Vaughan (2000), the public community colleges serve about ten million students per year—five million in credit courses and another five million in noncredit courses, activities, and programs.

The transfer function is of paramount importance to maintaining access to higher education by providing the lower-division coursework for a baccalaureate degree for those students who, immediately after high school, may be ineligible for admission to a four-year college or university. The open-access admissions philosophy and diversified curricula of public community colleges in the United States provide primary access to postsecondary education beyond the two-year college for diverse students.

The community college student who transfers to the four-year institution faces new psychological, academic, and environmental challenges. The academic challenges facing transfer students have been well documented. Keeley and House (1993) and Townsend (1993, 1995) have written that many students who transfer from community colleges to four-year institutions have trouble adjusting to the rigorous academic standards and are often faced with numerous other challenges upon enrolling in four-year institutions. This has been attributed, in part, to institutional differences in size, location, academic rigor, and competition among students (Holahan, Green, and Kelley, 1983; Laanan, 1996, 1998). The term *transfer shock* has been used to characterize the temporary dip in transfer students' academic performance (or grade point average—GPA) in the first or second

NEW DIRECTIONS FOR COMMUNITY COLLEGES, no. 114, Summer 2001 © John Wiley & Sons, Inc.

semester after transferring (Hills, 1965; Nolan and Hall, 1978; Webb, 1971; Williams, 1973).

Further research about the experiences of students at the community college who do transfer to senior institutions is necessary to determine the complexity of their adjustment process. Much of the research on community college students' transition to the four-year academic setting has focused on scholastic performance as measured by GPA. Other studies tend to compare transfer students with native students—that is, students who entered the four-year institution as freshmen—regarding various outcomes, such as time to degree, persistence, and graduation rates.

The research that examines the factors that contribute to post-transfer adjustment is very limited, especially in regard to students' emotional and psychological development at the four-year institution. A student's prior experience at the two-year college may influence both cognitive and affective outcomes at the senior institution. With a growing number of community college students transferring to senior institutions, more research is needed to better understand their academic preparation at the two-year institution and the extent to which their prior experiences facilitate or impede their educational progress at the four-year school.

Transfer Behavior

In 1997, the National Center for Education Statistics published a report entitled *Transfer Behavior Among Beginning Postsecondary Students: 1989–94.* Authored by McCormick and Carroll (1997), the report describes patterns of multiple institution attendance and transfer by students who first entered postsecondary education during the academic year 1989–90. Specifically, the data were drawn from the second follow-up of the 1990 Beginning Postsecondary Student Longitudinal Study (BPS), which was conducted in the spring of 1994 and was drawn from students who participated in the 1990 National Postsecondary Student Aid Study (NPSAS), which is a nationally representative cross-sectional survey of graduate and undergraduate students. The highlights of their analysis include the following:

- One out of four community college students indicated in 1989–90 that they were working toward a bachelor's degree (prospective transfers). Of this group, 39 percent transferred directly to a four-year institution by 1994.
- Among community college students identified as prospective transfers, those who enrolled full-time in their first year were about twice as likely as those who enrolled part-time to transfer to a four-year institution within five years—that is, 50 percent of full-timers transferred, compared with 26 percent of part-timers.
- Among community college beginners who transferred to a four-year institution, 65 percent transferred without a degree. About one out of three completed an associate's degree before transferring.

- On average, community college beginners who transferred to a four-year institution spent about twenty months at the first institution.
- While one out of four community college transfers had received a bachelor's degree by 1994, another 44 percent were still enrolled at a four-year institution, an overall persistence rate of 70 percent. This is comparable to the persistence rate among students who began at four-year institutions.
- The bachelor's degree attainment rate was much higher among the minority of community college transfers who completed an associate's degree before transferring: 43 percent of associate's degree completers had received a bachelor's degree by 1994, compared with 17 percent among those who transferred without any credential.

Post-Transfer Academic Performance

Four-year colleges and universities continue to be concerned about the academic success of students transferring from community colleges (Cross, 1968; Thornton, 1972). As a result, special attention has been paid to understanding how transfer students perform at senior institutions. For decades, studies have found that transfer students' grades were lower than those earned by upper-division students who had entered the university as freshmen (native students) (Cohen and Brawer, 1989).

In his review of research findings conducted from 1928 through 1964 relative to the success of junior college transfer students, Hills (1965) came up with three main conclusions: (1) transfer students should expect to suffer an appreciable drop in grades in the first semester after transfer, (2) transfer students' grades tend to improve in direct relation to their length of schooling, and (3) native students as a group are shown to perform better than the transfer students. Hills concluded that the transfer student who plans to earn a baccalaureate degree should be warned of the probability of suffering a potentially severe transfer shock. Furthermore, students will most likely encounter greater difficulty than native students and can expect to take longer to graduate.

Studies regarding the academic performance of transfer students have been concerned primarily with GPA because it is the most widely used index for admission of transfer students. Even with the abundance of research, conflicting results have been reported, ranging from the drop in GPA, called transfer shock, to an increase in GPA after transfer, sometimes called *transfer ecstasy*.

Most recently, an in-depth meta-analysis of transfer shock conducted by Diaz (1992) revealed sixty-two studies that reported the magnitude of GPA change. The studies showed that although community college transfer students in 79 percent of the studies experienced transfer shock, the magnitude of GPA change in most cases was one half of a grade point or less. Of the studies that showed that community college transfer students experienced transfer shock, 67 percent reported that students recover from transfer shock, usually within the first year after transfer. Significantly, 34 percent of these studies showed that community college transfer students recovered completely from transfer shock, 34 percent showed nearly complete recovery, and 32 percent showed partial recovery.

Transfer Adjustment Process

In addition to exploring the phenomenon of transfer shock, much of the recent research on community college transfer students has examined the transfer phenomenon from two other perspectives: (1) the student or institutional characteristics associated with transfer students' persistence at senior institutions and (2) the relationship between transfer students' academic performance at senior institutions and personal, demographic, or environmental characteristics (Graham and Hughes, 1994).

Comparisons with Native Students. Comparisons between the academic performance of transfer and native students have focused on attrition and persistence, graduation rates, and academic probation. Cohen and Brawer (1982) found that community college transfer students had lower GPAs and higher attrition rates than native students did. Richardson and Doucette (1980) used both GPAs and persistence rates to compare community college transfer students with native students and found differences among different types of receiving institutions. Graham and Dallam (1986) contrasted all transfer students (those from both four-year institutions and community colleges) with native students, using academic probation as an indicator of scholastic performance, and found that both groups of transfer students were more likely to end up on academic probation than native students were.

Personal, Demographic, or Environmental Characteristics. Research on transfer students has also sought to identify predictive variables associated with the persistence of transfer students at senior institutions. These studies applied models of student persistence in four-year colleges to transfer students. Using Tinto's constructs of social and academic integration (1975) as predictors of persistence in four-year colleges, Pascarella, Smart, and Ethington (1986) investigated the relevance of this model for transfer students' persistence. They found that the variables associated with social and academic integration played a role in the persistence of transfer students at four-year colleges and universities. Furthermore, Johnson (1987) examined the relationship between transfer students' persistence and four outcome measures: (1) the perceived practical value of education, (2) educational aspirations, (3) academic factors—that is, satisfaction, performance, self-concept, and integration, and (4) external factors, such as family, job, and finances. She found a relationship between persistence and academic satisfaction, performance, integration, and the perceived practical value of education. As a result of the preliminary investigations into the personal, demographic, and environmental characteristics of community college transfer students, the findings suggest that these factors may affect performance at senior institutions (Graham and Hughes, 1994).

Phlegar, Andrew, and McLaughlin (1981) conducted a study in an effort to clarify the conflicting results of the research on transfer students. Specifically, they sought to identify prior academic performance and personal and environmental variables that would predict the academic performance of transfer students at senior institutions. They found that students who met the key requirements of senior institutions—in math, science, and English—performed better than other transfers by two- to four-tenths of a grade point. Conversely, Hughes and Graham (1992) identified only one variable—class attendance at the community college—that distinguished between satisfactory and unsatisfactory performance during the first semester after transfer. For research projects focusing on personal, demographic, or environmental characteristics, Graham and Hughes (1994) argue that the relationship between these variables and academic performance over time needs to be assessed to determine whether transfer shock occurs mainly in the first semester of transfer, thus overshadowing the effects of variables that may predict long-term academic success.

Perspectives on College Adjustment

There is an abundance of research on student attrition. Many of these studies focus on factors that either positively or negatively affect students' decisions to stay in or drop out of college. However, only a handful of these studies have addressed aspects of college student adjustment. A few studies have included some measures that represent college adjustment directly in their models (Bennett and Okinaka, 1990; Chartrand, 1992), whereas others have simply made implications about adjustment. According to Hurtado, Carter, and Spuler (1996), college adjustment has not typically been the object of systematic study. Researchers do not rely on a single definition of college adjustment that might distinguish it from other constructs. In other words, because of the complexities of understanding student adjustment in college, scholars have advanced many constructs and frameworks yielding multiple theoretical perspectives.

Three main themes are prevalent in the research on college adjustment: psychological, environmental, and climate approaches. Of these, the majority of studies have addressed the psychological aspects of adjustment. In addition, the climate approach has received wide attention due to the changing demographics of students on college campuses.

Psychological Approaches. In his analysis of the Bean and Metzner Attrition Model (1985), Chartrand (1992) defined adjustment as institutional commitment, feelings of academic adjustment, and the absence of psychological distress. In another study, college adjustment is contrasted with *transitional trauma,* defined as the level of alienation a student experiences when unfamiliar with the norms, values, and expectations at the four-year institution (Bennett and Okinaka, 1990).

A popular perspective for examining college adjustment is to consider it as a type of psychological distress, along with personal, social, and academic dimensions. In a study examining minority freshmen, Smedley, Myers, and Harrell (1993) employed a stress-coping model to describe the adjustment process. These researchers used different instruments to measure chronic role strain, life events that cause stress, and minority status stressors in relation to three adjustment outcomes: psychological distress, feelings of well-being, and academic achievement. According to these authors, college adjustment is conceptualized as a function of student attributes, psychological and sociocultural stresses, and the strategies students use to cope with these stresses. They found that racial and ethnic minorities encounter additional stressors not typical of nonminority students. They conclude that stress derives from both internal sources and demographic composition and social climate on the campus.

Educational Environment. Another trend in studying college adjustment is to examine the influences of the educational environment. According to Hurtado, Carter, and Spuler (1996), assessing structural and climate characteristics of college campuses and the extent to which these factors may facilitate or impede a student's adjustment is critical to understanding the complex adjustment process. A major structural characteristic of a college or university is the faculty. Previous research suggests that spending quality time with faculty members positively affects a student's level of persistence, satisfaction, and academic performance (Astin, 1984, 1993; Pace, 1984, 1992; Tinto, 1987). Therefore, it is important to determine to what extent students interact with faculty members and spend quality time meeting with them outside of class.

Campus Climate. According to Hurtado, Carter, and Spuler (1996), a campus climate has many dimensions. It encompasses student interactions across race and ethnicity, perceptions of the climate for intergroup relations (racial and ethnic tension), experiences of overt discrimination, and the ethnic and racial diversity of the student body. Although the psychological perspectives mentioned earlier provide an important framework for studying college adjustment, the research literature also suggests that certain institutional characteristics can have an impact on an individual's adjustment to college. The extent to which a college is selective in the admissions process will have an effect on the academic adjustment of students. If the institution only accepts students of exceptional academic talent, as measured by SAT scores and GPA, students are forced to perform on a par with their counterparts. Hurtado (1992) found that both selective and private institutions tend to have distinct racial climates when compared to nonselective institutions. Another characteristic is college size. The size of the institution—for example, the size of its student body or its faculty—will contribute to students' feelings of anonymity, sense of community, or isolation (Chickering and Reisser, 1993). Furthermore, others contend that the impact of college size on college adjustment may have much to do with how students make sense of the environment, which is an important aspect of the early transition process (Attinasi, 1989).

Conclusion

Today, community college transfer programs play a critical role in providing access to individuals who desire to continue their education beyond a two-year institution. Students in the transfer pipeline have the opportunity to complete their general education requirements by participating in formalized articulation agreements and then transferring to the four-year institution of choice. Based on the research, transfer students are likely to experience a complex adjustment process—academically, socially, and psychologically—because of the environmental differences between two- and four-year institutions. Having an awareness of the expectations of the four-year school will facilitate a transfer student's successful transition and ultimate success in the completion of a bachelor's degree.

References

Astin, A. W. "Student Involvement: A Developmental Theory for Higher Education." *Journal of College Student Personnel*, 1984, *25*, 297–308.
Astin, A. W. *What Matters in College? Four Critical Years Revisited.* San Francisco: Jossey-Bass, 1993.
Attinasi, L. S., Jr. "Getting In: Mexican Americans' Perceptions of University Attendance and the Implications for Freshman Year Persistence." *Journal of Higher Education,* 1989, *60*, 247–277.
Bean, J. P., and Metzner, B. S. "A Conceptual Model of Nontraditional Undergraduate Student Attrition." *Review of Educational Research*, 1985, *55*, 485–539.
Bennett, C., and Okinaka, A. M. "Factors Related to Persistence Among Asian, Black, Hispanic, and White Undergraduates at a Predominantly White University: Comparison Between First- and Fourth-Year Cohorts." *Urban Review*, 1990, *22*, 33–60.
Chartrand, J. M. "An Empirical Test of a Model of Nontraditional Student Adjustment." *Journal of Counseling Psychology*, 1992, *39*, 193–202.
Chickering, A. W., and Reisser, L. *Education and Identity.* (2nd ed.) San Francisco: Jossey-Bass, 1993.
Cohen, A. M., and Brawer, F. B. *The American Community College.* San Francisco: Jossey-Bass, 1982.
Cohen, A. M., and Brawer, F. B. *The American Community College.* (2nd ed.) San Francisco: Jossey-Bass, 1989.
Cohen, A. M., and Brawer, F. B. *The American Community College.* (3rd ed.) San Francisco: Jossey-Bass, 1996.
Cross, K. P. *The Junior College Student: A Research Description.* Princeton, N.J.: Educational Testing Service, 1968.
Diaz, P. "Effects of Transfer on Academic Performance of Community College Students at the Four-Year Institution." *Community College Journal of Research and Practice,* 1992, *16*, 279–291.
Graham, S. W., and Dallam, J. "Academic Probation as a Measure of Performance: Contrasting Transfer Students to Native Students." *Community/Junior College Quarterly of Research and Practice*, 1986, *10*, 23–24.

Graham, S. W., and Hughes, J. A. "Moving Down the Road: Community College Students' Academic Performance at the University." *Community College Journal of Research and Practice,* 1994, *18,* 449–464.

Hills, J. "Transfer Shock: The Academic Performance of the Junior College Transfer." *Journal of Experimental Education,* 1965, *33,* 201–216.

Holahan, C. K., Green, J. L., and Kelley, H. P. "A Six-Year Longitudinal Analysis of Transfer Student Performance and Retention." *Journal of College Student Personnel,* 1983, *24,* 305–310.

Hughes, J. A., and Graham, S. W. "Academic Performance and Background Characteristics Among Community College Transfer Students." *Community/Junior College Quarterly of Research and Practice,* 1992, *16,* 35–46.

Hurtado, S. "The Campus Racial Climate: Contexts for Conflict." *Journal of Higher Education,* 1992, *63,* 539–569.

Hurtado, S., Carter, D. F., and Spuler, A. "Latino Student Transition to College: Assessing Difficulties and Factors in Successful College Adjustment." *Research in Higher Education,* 1996, *37,* 135–157.

Johnson, N. T. "Academic Factors That Affect Transfer Student Persistence." *Journal of College Student Personnel,* 1987, *28,* 323–329.

Keeley, E. J., and House, J. D. "Transfer Shock Revisited: A Longitudinal Study of Transfer Academic Performance." Paper presented at the annual forum of the Association for Institutional Research, Chicago, May 1993.

Laanan, F. S. "Making the Transition: Understanding the Adjustment Process of Community College Transfer Students." *Community College Review,* 1996, 23(4), 69–84.

Laanan, F. S. "Beyond Transfer Shock: A Study of Students' College Experiences and Adjustment Processes at UCLA." Unpublished doctoral dissertation, Graduate School of Education and Information Studies, University of California, Los Angeles, 1998.

McCormick, A. C., and Carroll, C. D. *Transfer Behavior Among Beginning Postsecondary Students, 1989–94.* Washington, D.C.: U.S. Department of Education, 1997. (ED 408 929)

Nolan, E. J., and Hall, D. L. "Academic Performance of the Community College Transfer Student: A Five-Year Follow-Up Study." *Journal of College Student Personnel,* 1978, *19,* 543–548.

Pace, C. R. *Measuring the Quality of College Student Experiences.* Los Angeles: Center for the Study of Evaluation, University of California, 1984.

Pace, C. R. *College Student Experiences Questionnaire: Norms for the Third Edition, 1990.* Los Angeles: Center for the Study of Evaluation, University of California, 1992.

Pascarella, E., Smart, J., and Ethington, C. "Long-Term Persistence of Two-Year College Students." *Research in Higher Education,* 1986, *24,* 47–71.

Phlegar, A. G., Andrew, L. D., and McLaughlin, G. W. "Explaining the Academic Performance of Community College Students Who Transfer to a Senior Institution." *Research in Higher Education,* 1981, *15,* 99–108.

Richardson, R. C., Jr., and Doucette, D. S. *Persistence, Performance, and Degree Achievement of Arizona's Community College Transfers in Arizona's Public Universities.* 1980. (ED 197 785)

Smedley, B. D., Myers, H. F., and Harrell, S. P. "Minority-Status Stresses and the College Adjustment of Ethnic Minority Freshmen." *Journal of Higher Education,* 1993, *64,* 434–452.

Thornton, J. W., Jr. *The Community Junior College.* (3rd ed.) New York: Wiley, 1972.

Tinto, V. "Dropout from Higher Education: A Theoretical Synthesis of Recent Research." *Review of Higher Education,* 1975, *63,* 603–618.

Tinto, V. *Leaving College: Rethinking the Causes and Cures of Student Attrition.* Chicago: University of Chicago Press, 1987.

Townsend, B. K. "University Practices That Hinder the Academic Success of Community College Transfer Students." Paper presented at the annual meeting of the Association for the Study of Higher Education, Pittsburgh, Pa., Nov. 1993.

Townsend, B. K. "Community College Transfer Students: A Case Study of Survival." *Review of Higher Education*, 1995, *18*, 175–193.

Vaughan, G. B. *The Community College Story*. (2nd ed.) Washington, D.C.: Community College Press, 2000.

Webb, S. "Estimated Effects of Four Factors on Academic Performance Before and After Transfer." *Journal of Experimental Education*, 1971, *39*, 78–84.

Williams, R. "Transfer Shock as Seen from a Student's Point of View." *College and University*, 1973, *48*, 320–321.

FRANKIE SANTOS LAANAN is assistant professor of community college leadership in the Department of Human Resource Education at the University of Illinois at Urbana-Champaign.

2

The extent to which community college students make the transition from two- to four-year institutions is contingent on the cooperation of these institutions. This chapter examines the creation of transfer centers and other initiatives to address the challenges in the transfer process.

Institutional Responses to Barriers to the Transfer Process

Eboni M. Zamani

Community colleges are often viewed as bridging the gap in baccalaureate degree attainment for many students. Following the 1970s decline, the transfer rate has remained low during the 1980s and 1990s, ranging between 20 and 25 percent. The literature suggests that community colleges can reinforce their position in the educational pipeline by emphasizing transfer within their home institutions (Palmer, 1987; Prager, 1992). Recent legislation and foundation activities support collaborations and partnerships between institutional two- and four-year institutions as a means of enhancing the transfer rate. One way that community colleges have sought to augment transfer rates, address barriers, and better facilitate transition between the two tiers has been through the development of transfer centers and institutes.

Barriers to Transfer

Many community college students intend to transfer to four-year colleges and universities; however, only 22 percent successfully do so (McCormick and Carroll, 1997). For the last two decades, studies examining the transfer function have revealed that the proportion of two-year students actually transferring is deficient and that differential rates of transfer exist between racial, ethnic, and socioeconomic groups. Of particular concern is the low college-going rate among high school graduates of racially and ethnically diverse heritage (Stewart, 1988). Low-income and non-Asian minority students have lower transfer and program completion rates, compared with their white counterparts from families with higher annual income (Bender, 1991; Brint and Karabel, 1989; Cohen, 1988; Richardson and Skinner, 1992). Furthermore,

NEW DIRECTIONS FOR COMMUNITY COLLEGES, no. 114, Summer 2001   © John Wiley & Sons, Inc.

research results suggest that collegians who begin postsecondary education at two-year institutions are less likely to earn baccalaureate degrees, particularly African American and Hispanic community college students (Dougherty, 1992; Pascarella and others, 1998; Pincus and Archer, 1989; Velez, 1985).

There are various explanations as to why the progress of community college students may stagnate and how transfer to four-year institutions has been hindered. The lack of financial resources is one of many barriers facing community college students who are attending, persisting, and, in some cases, ultimately transferring to four-year institutions (McDonough, 1997). Student aid has shifted so that fewer grant dollars are awarded, whereas federal student loans have increased. Students coming from low socioeconomic backgrounds are at a disadvantage, as the costs associated with higher education may prohibit even the most talented two-year students from successfully transferring into a baccalaureate degree program (Stewart, 1988). In addition, Stewart suggests that the lack of academic preparation of many entering community college students often serves to discourage their aspirations.

Although student financial background and academic readiness for college-level work may act against some students, institutional factors also place hurdles in the path of students desiring to transfer to four-year institutions. For example, undergraduate retention and matriculation are often affected by institutional characteristics, such as campus climate and culture. The installation of transfer centers is an institutional response that can address academic preparation for baccalaureate programs through encouraging two- and four-year institutional relationships and underscoring the importance of collegiate culture.

Dougherty (1994) asserts that the transfer function within community colleges is ineffective due to an influx of underprepared students, coupled with a less collegiate environment and culture. Unlike four-year institutions that primarily enroll traditional-aged students, who then reside in campus dormitories, the community college culture is nonresidential. Two-year students at commuter campuses are typically on campus less often than are students at four-year institutions because of work responsibilities; they attempt fewer credit hours and they interact with faculty members less as a result of residing away from the college (Rice, 1990). It is estimated that residential students are 43 percent more likely to persist and complete degree requirements than are commuter students (Velez, 1985). Hence, establishing alternate learning communities at the two-year level may help increase the likelihood of student matriculation.

Related to the relative amount of transfer activity are student characteristics and educational aspirations. Students within each type of institution who aspire to baccalaureate degrees or higher were up to three times as likely to transfer than those not expecting to complete a bachelor's degree (McCormick and Carroll, 1997). It has been noted in the literature that private four-year colleges and universities may afford more opportunities to gain entrance for those who fall short of meeting admissions standards at public universities (Glass and Bunn, 1998).

In addition to institutional type, poor student transitions between two- and four-year institutions often reflect a lack of student-college fit. The institutional environment is an important factor in the rate of student transfer and success in earning a bachelor's degree. More specifically, students of color may perceive homogenous institutional environments to be noninclusive and lacking a commitment to fostering cultural pluralism, multicultural curriculum, and campus diversity (Haralson, 1996). With a greater number of underrepresented African American and Hispanic students attending community colleges, institutional policies and programs intended to encourage inclusion and invigorate minority student transfer in particular are imperative.

Addressing Emerging Problems: Transfer Center Outgrowth

The transfer process increases educational opportunity and access beyond two-year institutions; however, paradoxically, it also immobilizes many students, as policies related to the movement of students between community colleges and four-year colleges/universities are inconsistent or nonexistent. For example, there has been considerable growth in the rate of transfer to senior institutions among community college students enrolled in professional and vocational-technical programs (Bender, 1990; Cohen and Brawer, 1996; Dougherty, 1992). Likewise, roughly three-fourths of all vocational-technical students desire baccalaureate degrees (Dougherty, 1992; Hunter and Sheldon, 1980). However, the transferability of career and vocational courses is problematic for those intending to earn baccalaureate degrees, since the articulation of such course credits is inconsistent between two- and four-year institutions (Keener, 1994).

According to Tobolowsky (1998), articulation has become increasingly complex and is no longer a vertical process, as multidirectional student movement calls for a range of transfer services. Cohen and Brawer (1996) describe the back-and-forth movement of college students as being illustrative of articulation agreements that coordinate course offerings, formalize admissions requirements in correspondence to programs of study, and simplify transfer planning. Articulation encompasses (1) formal, legally binding agreements, (2) state system transfer policies, and (3) voluntary arrangements between two- and four-year colleges (Cohen, 1988). Emphasis on articulation and transfer are of paramount concern, as previous levels of cooperation among sectors have not moved more students—African American and Hispanic, in particular—through the educational pipeline.

Facilitating Policy and Programmatic Changes

To address some of the recurring challenges to the transfer process, the State of California revised its higher education master plan in 1985. The Master Plan for Higher Education in California reflected legislation (AB 1725) that was passed to reform coordination with the community college system

(Academic Senate for California Community Colleges, 1996; Nussbaum, 1997). Moreover, Senate Bill 121 was signed in 1991, establishing that California community colleges, the University of California system, and the California State University system are jointly accountable for instituting a solid transfer function and for placing emphasis on raising the rate of transfer among historically underrepresented students (Academic Senate for California Community Colleges, 1996).

In response to Senate Bill 121, California Community Colleges and the University of California produced an official memorandum of understanding that reiterates the shared responsibility of each party to provide access and opportunities to those with transfer intentions and baccalaureate degree aspirations (Nussbaum, 1997). Delineated in the memorandum are nine target areas: (1) to improve articulation agreements by initiating the California Articulation Number System (CANS systemwide course sequencing), (2) to use ASSIST (Articulation System Stimulating Interinstitutional Student Transfer) as the official statewide repository for articulation information and data, (3) to reinvigorate transfer center partnerships, (4) to enhance transfer alliances to ensure a seamless transition for students, (5) to increase additional part-time attendance options at the University of California in order to meet the needs of part-time transfer students, (6) to develop a baccalaureate financial aid package that meets transfer students' needs for degree completion at four-year institutions, (7) to heighten outreach activities in an effort to recruit and attract students seeking transfer, (8) to monitor and evaluate transfer activities through additional data collection and information exchange, and (9) to enhance cooperative admissions programs that involve eligible high school graduates who would like the option of attending a community college and later transferring to the University of California (Nussbaum, 1997).

Acknowledging the importance of collaborative efforts between two- and four-year institutions of higher learning, the Ford Foundation gave a grant to the National Center for Educational Alliances, formerly the National Center for Urban Partnerships. In 1991, the center was established to manage the Ford Foundation's Urban Partnership Program, which originated in response to the growing number of underprepared, underrepresented, low-income students with degree aspirations extending beyond the community college level (McGrath and Van Buskirk, 1998). The Urban Community College Transfer Opportunities Grant created sixteen urban site partnerships, including the Bronx, Chicago, Los Angeles, Miami, and Phoenix. Administered in the early 1990s, the grant brought about the development of transfer centers to address issues surrounding articulation. Additionally, transfer centers prioritized support services to meet transfer-track student needs and enhance transitions between tiers for the transfer population.

Affiliated with the National Center for Urban Partnerships, the Memphis Center for Urban Partnerships (MCUP) comprises the University of Memphis,

LeMoyne-Owen College, Shelby State Community College, and Memphis City Schools, which have unified to build pathways for increasing access and academic achievement for at-risk students. More specifically, the MCUP targets increasing college attendance and completion rates among African American students in response to high secondary attrition rates, poverty, and low college enrollment. MCUP has been effective in creating change in the community that is consistent with its mission.

The African American Scholars Program (AASP) helps students from Frayser and Westside High School who are attending Shelby State Community College transfer to four-year colleges and universities. The goal of AASP is to make the transition from high school to college and from a two-year to a four-year college smoother. This has been accomplished through partial funds received from the Ford Foundation to create an African American Transfer Center. The center assists with career planning, provides academic counseling, and hosts retention and academic skills workshops and motivational guest lectures (Memphis Center for Urban Partnerships, Feb. 2001). As a result of the educational service components, students have an increased responsiveness and understanding of skills necessary for college success. Finally, although the Ford Foundation urban partnership grant was awarded to several cities, there is little literature examining the majority of affected states with regard to program activities and effectiveness. Nevertheless, each of the National Center for Educational Alliances cities has made use of Ford Foundation grant dollars to aid inner-city students in overcoming the hurdles associated with being from a disenfranchised group by devising strategies to improve student learning and subsequent educational success.

Successful Programs Addressing Student Transfer

Community colleges primarily face the difficulty of determining how to best facilitate student transfer to senior-level postsecondary institutions. Although national transfer rates could stand much improvement, there has been inventiveness on the part of some two- and four-year institutions to collaborate in promoting and encouraging the transition between tiers, particularly for underrepresented students. In response to some of the challenges associated with transfer and articulation, the following section of this chapter highlights programmatic efforts and policy initiatives that speak to student progression from two- to four-year colleges.

Current literature examining transfer provides statistics that indicate the small percentage of transfer-track students who actually earn associate's degrees, the smaller number of students who transfer to four-year institutions, and the even smaller number who persist toward the bachelor's degree (Bender, 1991; Brint and Karabel, 1989; Dougherty, 1994; McCormick and Carroll, 1997). As a result, there is a need for two- and four-year colleges to work in partnership to create and optimize transfer opportunities.

One program that has met the challenge is the Summer Scholars Transfer Institute (SSTI). Created in 1993, SSTI is a team approach involving Santa Ana College, numerous Los Angeles community colleges, and the University of California at Irvine to provide intervention for underrepresented students (McGrath and Van Buskirk, 1998). Sponsored by the National Center for Educational Alliances, the program focuses on assisting low-income students—predominantly African American and Hispanic students—at urban community colleges.

Students taking part in the program are undecided as to whether they intend to continue beyond their two-year institutions. Students are required to hold a minimum GPA of 2.0, meet eligibility for Freshman Composition, and have taken fewer than 30 credit units. Unique by design, SSTI works with roughly 150 first-generation students annually, during the summer months. This eleven-day residential program is designed to blend institutional cultures of the participating colleges while structuring condensed academic courses and social support systems to ensure success (McGrath and Van Buskirk, 1998). Students have the option to take one of five courses that are 3 credit hours each. The initial class meeting is scheduled one month prior to the start of the institute, at which time students receive an overview of the course by the instructor and substantial reading and writing assignments. Students attend class during the daytime for the eleven days and participate in study groups throughout the evening and late-night hours. A university faculty member and a community college counselor lead courses, with teaching assistants being assigned to assist in communication between students and staff members.

McGrath and Van Buskirk's qualitative examination (1998) of the SSTI provides rich description and anecdotal commentaries, indicating the effectiveness of this approach. The authors report that from 1993 to 1998 the number of underrepresented students transferring to the University of California from Santa Ana College doubled, moving Santa Ana College from 44th to 9th place statewide for the number of Hispanic transfer students to the University of California system. In addition, 95 percent of all students have successfully completed the general education course taken under the auspices of SSTI, in contrast with the 60 percent who complete it on campus.

The Illinois Board of Higher Education provided funding to twenty-five community colleges to operate minority transfer centers. Each center has a director at the helm to oversee all activities that include developing articulation agreements with four-year institutions. It is estimated that over twenty-five thousand students are served by these minority transfer centers annually. As a result of these efforts, transfer rates for African American and Hispanic community college students increased by 12.7 and 38.6 percent, respectively, from 1990 to 1994. In addition, there was a 61.3 percent increase during the same period in transfers of Hispanic community college students to private institutions. Participating centers reported an increase of 3.4 percent in total community college student transfers (Illinois Community College Board, 1996).

Oakton Community College in Illinois has a high percentage of first-generation college students, many of whom are considering further education. Every semester, approximately 65 percent of Oakton's students enroll in courses with the intention of transferring to a senior-level college or university. As one of the twenty-five colleges that received a grant from the Illinois Board of Higher Education to establish a transfer center, Oakton offers workshops, plans campus visits to four-year institutions, and advises students regarding course of study, financial aid, and scholarships (Oakton Community College, 1997).

The University of California at Davis, in conjunction with the Los Rios Community College District, funded a transfer opportunity program with nine Northern California community colleges to extend outreach efforts and transfer services. In a related program, the Los Rios Community College transfer centers sponsored a College Transfer Day to inform students of transfer issues and to allow them to discuss admissions concerns and programs of study with university representatives (Case, 1999). The University of California at Davis has also worked closely with the California Community Colleges to offer early academic outreach programs at elementary, middle, and secondary schools in seventeen school districts. The aim of the program is to give school officials, teachers, parents, and, most of all, students information regarding college preparation and transfer readiness. Other efforts by the UC system and California Community Colleges that are making significant contributions to the improvement of the transfer process include the Math, Engineering, Science Achievement/California Community College Program (MESA/CCCP)—a transfer support program for nontraditional students in the sciences, faculty-to-faculty articulation dialogues, a transfer student recruitment campaign on the Web, and Ensuring Transfer Success Counselor Institutes (ETSCI) (Case, 1999).

The transfer center at Glendale Community College (GCC) combined forces with seven other Los Angeles community colleges in writing a grant to receive funding from the Office of the Chancellor to underwrite the airfare for students' campus visits to the University of San Francisco, San Francisco State University, UC Berkeley, and UC Davis. Like other community colleges that are interested in boosting transfer, the transfer center at Glendale held Transfer Day Fairs in addition to having outreach advisers from UCLA join the center staff to host an orientation and reception for Glendale students accepted to UCLA (Glendale Community College, 1998). As a result of the wide array of transfer services provided by the center, Glendale Community College ranks second among the top transfer institutions sending students to UCLA, with 52 percent of the GCC applicants gaining admission.

Conclusions and Recommendations for Enhancing Transfer

As flaws in the transfer process have been identified, innovative programs and policies to revive the transfer function within community colleges have been implemented. University and community college partnerships have facilitated smooth transitions through research, articulation arrangements, and campus programming—such as SSTI, transfer fairs, and four-year campus visits.

Community colleges must continue to strive to be forerunners at recognizing impediments to student progression and successful transfer. This responsibility should not lie solely with the two-year sector, as often the blame for lack of success in the transfer process is placed on community colleges. Two- and four-year institutions must be responsive and aggressive in addressing the role of transfer in producing upward mobility. Academic support professionals at community colleges and senior institutions can address challenges to the transfer function by instituting on-site transfer centers, establishing cooperative admissions agreements, extending outreach activities, clarifying articulation agreements, hosting transfer informational sessions, conducting four-year campus tours, and creating innovative approaches to academic skills acquisition. Newer approaches that have developed include the consideration of redefining student success, services to assist reverse transfer student concerns, and orientation programs that convey how to make the transition from an open to a selective system of admissions in an effort to curb transfer shock (Cejda, 1997; Laanan, 1996; Townsend, 2000).

With affirmative action under attack, the transfer function should be considered one means of recruiting and admitting diverse students (Zamani, forthcoming). Thus, colleges and universities can use the transfer function to reposition themselves to more wholly represent their respective communities and reach parity with regard to race, ethnicity, gender, and social class standing.

References

Academic Senate for California Community Colleges. *Toward Increased Student Success: Transfer as an Institutional Commitment.* Sacramento: Academic Senate for California Community Colleges, 1996. (ED 403 007)

Bender, L. W. *Spotlight on the Transfer Function: A National Study of State Policies and Practices.* Washington, D.C.: American Association of Community and Junior Colleges, 1990. (ED 317 246)

Bender, L. W. "Minority Transfer: A National and State Legislative Perspective." In D. Angel and A. Barrera (eds.), *Rekindling Minority Enrollment.* New Directions for Community Colleges, no. 74. San Francisco: Jossey-Bass, 1991.

Brint, S., and Karabel, J. "American Education, Meritocratic Ideology, and the Legitimization of Inequality: The Community College and the Problem of American Exceptionalism." *Higher Education,* 1989, *18,* 725–735.

Case, L. B. *Transfer Opportunity Program: Written Testimony to the Little Hoover Commission Public Hearing on Community Colleges.* Sacramento, Calif.: Los Rios Community College District, 1999. (ED 427 824)

Cejda, B. D. "An Examination of Transfer Shock in Academic Disciplines." *Community College Journal of Research and Practice*, 1997, *21*, 279–288.

Cohen, A. M. "Degree Achievement by Minorities in Community Colleges." *Review of Higher Education*, 1988, *11*, 383–402.

Cohen, A. M., and Brawer, F. B. *The American Community College.* (3rd ed.) San Francisco: Jossey-Bass, 1996.

Dougherty, K. J. "Community Colleges and Baccalaureate Attainment." *Journal of Higher Education*, 1992, *63*, 188–214.

Dougherty, K. J. *The Contradictory College: The Conflicting Origins, Impacts, and Future of the Community College.* Albany: State University of New York Press, 1994.

Glass, J. C., Jr., and Bunn, C. E. "Length of Time Required to Graduate for Community College Students Transferring to Senior Institutions." *Community College Journal of Research and Practice*, 1998, *22*, 239–263.

Glendale Community College. *College Services Annual Report, 1997–1998.* Glendale, Calif.: Glendale Community College, 1998. (ED 426 747)

Haralson, M., Jr. "Survival Factors for Black Students on Predominantly White Campuses." Paper presented at the annual meeting of the National Association of Student Personnel Administrators, Atlanta, Ga., 1996. (ED 402 515)

Hunter, R., and Sheldon, M. S. *Statewide Longitudinal Study: Report on Academic Year 1979–80, Part 3: Fall Results.* Woodland, Hills, Calif.: Los Angeles Pierce College, 1980. (ED 188 714)

Illinois Community College Board. *Community College Programs and Services for Special Populations and Underrepresented Groups, Fiscal Year 1995.* Springfield: Illinois Community College Board, 1996. (ED 395 621)

Keener, B. J. "Capturing the Community College Market." *Currents*, 1994, *20*(5), 38–43.

Laanan, F. S. Making the Transition: Understanding the Adjustment Process of Community College Transfer Students. *Community College Review*, 1996, *23*(4), 69–84.

McCormick, A. C., and Carroll, C. D. *Transfer Behavior Among Beginning Postsecondary Students, 1989–94.* Washington, D.C.: U.S. Department of Education, 1997. (ED 408 929)

McDonough, P. M. *Choosing Colleges: How Social Class and Schools Structure Opportunity.* Albany: State University of New York Press, 1997.

McGrath, D., and Van Buskirk, W. *Si, Se Puede = Yes, It Can Be Done: The Summer Scholars Transfer Institute Collaborating to Promote Access and Achievement.* New York: National Center for Urban Partnerships, 1998. (ED 425 775)

"Memphis Center for Urban Partnerships." [http://www.people.memphis.edu/~coe_mcup]. Feb. 2001.

Nussbaum, T. J. *Enhancing Student Transfer: A Memorandum of Understanding Between the California Community Colleges and the University of California.* Sacramento: California Community Colleges Office of the Chancellor, 1997. (ED 414 965)

Oakton Community College. *Oakton Community College Annual Report to the Community, Fiscal Year 1997.* Des Plaines, Ill.: Oakton Community College, 1997. (ED 413 951)

Palmer, J. "Bolstering the Community College Transfer Function: An ERIC Review." *Community College Review*, 1987, *14*(3), 53–63.

Pascarella, E. T., and others. "Does Work Inhibit Cognitive Development During College?" *Educational Evaluation and Policy Analysis*, 1988, *20*, 75–93.

Pincus, F., and Archer, E. *Bridges to Opportunity: Are Community Colleges Meeting the Transfer Needs of Minority Students?* New York: Academy for Educational Development and College Entrance Examination Board, 1989.

Prager, C. "Accreditation and Transfer: Mitigating Elitism." In B. W. Dziech and W. R. Vilter (eds.), *Prisoners of Elitism: The Community College's Struggle for Stature.* New Directions for Community Colleges, no. 78. San Francisco: Jossey-Bass, 1992.

Rice, R. L. "Commuter Students." In M. L. Upcraft and J. N. Gardner (eds.), *The Freshman-Year Experience: Helping Students Survive and Succeed in College.* San Francisco: Jossey-Bass, 1990.

Richardson, R. C., and Skinner, E. F. "Helping First-Generation Minority Students Achieve Degrees." In L. S. Zwerling and H. B. London (eds.), *First-Generation Students: Confronting the Cultural Issues.* New Directions for Community Colleges, no. 80. San Francisco: Jossey-Bass, 1992.

Stewart, D. M. "Overcoming the Barriers to Successful Participation by Minorities." *Review of Higher Education,* 1988, *11,* 329–336.

Tobolowsky, B. "Improving Transfer and Articulation Policies." *ERIC Clearinghouse for Community Colleges Digest,* Mar. 1998.

Townsend, B. A. "Transfer Students' Institutional Attendance Patterns: A Case Study." *College and University,* 2000, *76,* 21–24.

Velez, W. "Finishing College: The Effects of College Type." *Sociology of Education,* 1985, *58,* 191–200.

Zamani, E. M. "Affirmative Action Attitudes of African American Community College Students: The Impact of Educational Aspirations, Self-Interest, and Racial Affect." In C. C. Yeakey, R. D. Henderson, and M. Shujaa (eds.), *Research on African American Education.* Vol. 1. Greenwich, Conn.: Information Age, forthcoming.

EBONI M. ZAMANI is assistant professor of higher education administration at West Virginia University.

3

This chapter traces the design and development of the San Diego City College Honors Program and its successful implementation of intersegmental transfer agreements— chief among them being the Transfer Alliance Program (TAP), with the University of California, Los Angeles (UCLA). It describes the recent historical context in which community college honors programs took on a strong leadership role in addressing deep systemic problems in the transfer function in California, a role that continues to this day. This chapter identifies the pivotal contributions of intersegmental transfer agreements like TAP in the development of honors programs at community colleges, and it emphasizes their implications for college students and faculty members.

Honors Programs: A Case Study of Transfer Preparation

Herald R. Kane

The founding of the San Diego Community College District (SDCCD) Honors Program in 1986 came at a time when it bordered on heretical to mention "honors" and "community colleges" in the same breath. Untoward political events and major demographic shifts over the previous decade had dramatically affected the colleges, causing operational changes that seriously eroded public confidence that they could supply students who would be successful after transfer, especially at the University of California (UC). Some colleges showed signs of becoming resigned to their newly emphasized roles of remediation and occupational instruction, and they began to devote less energy and resources to their assigned transfer function.

In the early 1980s, a refreshing new dialogue between California's university and community college segments set out a new ground of collaboration that seemed promising to all concerned. The University of California would implement new measures of assurance that qualified transfers from the community colleges would be welcomed at the junior level; the colleges in return would agree to provide specially "enriched" lower-division academic preparation to prospective transfer students, assuaging the concerns that those students would not succeed at the four-year institution.

San Diego City College was invited to join the UCLA Transfer Alliance Program (TAP) in 1991, after five years of successful operation of an honors program. Interestingly, it was both the earlier prospect of membership in TAP and the actual membership itself that played an important role in consolidating support for honors among administrators, faculty members, and students at City College. Over a decade later, the relationship with UCLA ripened into an effective partnership with a high level of trust and a gratifying openness to communication in support of individual students on their way through the transfer process.

Throughout the 1990s, the San Diego City College Honors Program elaborated and strengthened its role in enriching the academic and personal growth of its students and faculty members. Its profile both within and beyond the campus community has been buoyed not only by its intersegmental transfer agreements (TAP is now one of over a dozen), but also by its collaboration with regional and national organizations devoted to the widely expanded "honors movement."

In its next decade, the program aspires to a leading role in attracting many more talented and motivated students to City College and contributing to a spirit and practice of excellence across the entire college curriculum. Fifteen years of enhancing both transfer preparedness and occupational readiness of students has positioned the honors program to take a leadership role in current discussions exploring statewide transfer agreements with all campuses of the University of California and California State University systems. And finally, the commitment to imbed "global awareness and competencies" in the honors curriculum, as described later in this chapter, will encourage and equip students to reach beyond regional and national boundaries to enrich their educational experiences even more.

Transfer: A Classic Conundrum

Honors programs have been known among American community colleges for some time (Bentley-Baker, 1983)—albeit, until the mid-1980s, only among an almost vanishing minority of colleges responding to occasional surveys. For example, one such survey conducted for the American Association of Community and Junior Colleges counted 644 responding colleges but only 47 honors programs (Piland and Gould, 1982). The National Collegiate Honors Council (NCHC), arguably the current de facto leader in defining and promoting the national honors movement, had by 1981 dissolved its Standing Committee on Honors in the Two-Year College for apparent lack of interest and participation (Bentley-Baker, 1983).

From these modest beginnings, the revival and rapid expansion of interest in honors in the community colleges have continued without interruption for nearly two decades. The reasons for the dramatic "comeback" are many and interesting. In this chapter, particular emphasis is placed, of course, on the ways in which the pressure for transfer improvement prompted and promoted such a movement.

University-Devised Transfer Incentive Programs. The decade of the 1970s was a difficult one for the transfer function in California. Decline in the transfer rates was inexorable and alarming. For the nine-campus University of California system there was a 40 percent drop-off in the period of 1975 to 1981 (Wilbur, 1996). Critics proclaimed an imbedded public perception that the community colleges had become lesser, even unworthy, institutions for the serious academic student (Wilbur, 1996). Perhaps no other stakeholder than the University itself, with the prestige and political power to set the agenda for higher education, could rescue the colleges from this unhappy condition. Simply stimulating the transfer rate by accepting greater numbers of transfers had already been tried and found wanting, because real deficiencies in student preparation to do upper-division work were being reported (Wilbur, 1996). Perhaps the University could link its acceptance of more transfer students to a new, more proactive involvement in stimulating the academic preparation of "its own students-to-be" while they were still in the community college system.

By the mid-1980s, new courtships and relationships between UC campuses and groups of their feeder community colleges began to emerge. UC Davis offered local community college students a signed, individualized guarantee of admission at the junior level if they committed themselves to follow a detailed educational plan with periodic monitoring by an academic counselor. They would also have to complete 56 units of lower-division preparation for the major and general education requirements, with a minimum grade point average (GPA) of 2.40. Several other campuses of the University implemented similar plans, in accordance with the expressed policy of the UC President's Office, shaping them to fit their own student profile and capacity for outreach. Copies of a glossy, warmly written brochure entitled "Answers for Transfer" began to appear in colorful profusion on community college campuses across the state. The University's efforts to reach across the divide were growing.

Within the typical transfer agreement, the community college need only provide traditional academic counseling and educational planning services to qualified individual students; the local UC campus would establish a marginally more active presence on the community college campus, providing pretransfer guidance, along with informational materials on academic programs. Transfer workshops for college counselors and on-campus student visitation opportunities could be conducted periodically by admissions officers of the University and be overseen by its Office of Undergraduate Admissions and Relations with Schools. Beyond an incremental increase in outreach effort by the University, these agreements brought little new insight or creative change to the troubled transfer situation. Certainly, they inspired no profound changes in either institution, or in the ways that they related to each other.

Birth of the UCLA Transfer Alliance Program (TAP). TAP has provided perhaps the best model to date of a comprehensive intersegmental mechanism for community college-to-university transfer (Clemons, Kane, and McLeod, 1995). No other transfer agreement—on any other campus of the University of California—anticipated the breadth and depth of the effort it took to launch the Transfer Alliance Program. UCLA academic leaders first established and infused with meaningful levels of financial and personnel resources a new Center for Academic Interinstitutional Programs (CAIP). CAIP was then enjoined to stimulate linkages among UCLA faculty members and their community college and high school counterparts in curriculum review and alignment. Third, the center's directors took the lead in systematically developing a network of working relationships between community college administrators and faculty members and their UCLA counterparts, gradually building a level of trust that released creative problem-solving energies from all concerned. And fourth, capping several years of team building between institutions and addressing the concerns of detractors within each segment, they finally delivered the first version of the Transfer Alliance Program, in 1985.

Indicators of the TAP Philosophy. The goal of the new program was deceptively simple: to contribute to the solution of a nagging problem in transfer and persistence rates of community college students moving to UCLA. This was to be accomplished by offering priority admission consideration to students who completed an enriched lower-division curriculum, including general education requirements and preparation courses for the intended major. But the real wisdom of TAP lay at a much deeper level—namely, in the realization that bonds among people committed to collaboration with their distant counterparts at other institutions, all in the service of needy students, supplied the cohesion necessary to hold the agreement together over time.

UCLA's chancellor and senior administrators had already fought hard within the statewide UC structure to secure approval for extending such a profound measure of openness to the community colleges. They had proclaimed UCLA's belief in two-year college students, offering for the first time a deliberate acknowledgment that our students were, indeed, UCLA students, save only for the short-term growth and tempering experiences currently in progress at the two-year institutions. Their conviction assuaged a real concern that the statewide UC admission policy was going to be affected in some unknown and potentially troublesome ways.

Furthermore, implementation of TAP at a two-year college had the potential to profoundly and permanently affect several aspects of how that college conceived and delivered its transfer curriculum. Benefits were sure to extend beyond the student participants themselves. Faculty and institutional development would certainly follow from the new levels of attention devoted to academic improvement and from new collaborations among faculty members, counselors, and other student support services personnel at the college itself.

Anatomy of a TAP Program at the Two-Year College. Well beyond the scope of the incentive contracts signed by some UC campuses and individual transfer aspirants enrolled at the two-year college, TAP crystallized the collaboration between UCLA and the college at several levels of each institution. A 1991 version of the UCLA document "Elements of a Transfer Alliance Program" laid out across three domains the considerable expectations to be met by a college aspiring to join TAP—by then a group of about a dozen institutions.

To address structural and support issues, the two-year college president was asked to write a letter assuring UCLA of the desirability of a TAP affiliation and committing the college to support the program administratively. There was to be appropriate release time for a classroom faculty member (specifically not a counselor or administrator) to coordinate the program and represent the college on the UCLA TAP council of directors at its quarterly meetings. There had to be an assurance that academic enrichment would be imbedded in the transfer curriculum; for many colleges, that was the first, and perhaps most forceful, impetus they had had for the development of an "honors program," or some equivalent that met TAP standards. The TAP or honors program should report directly to an academic dean or vice president and be appropriately represented in the college governance process. There were additional recommendations for a collegewide advisory group, including faculty members, administrators, and students, as well as clerical support, office space, and student space appropriate to the size of the TAP or honors program. Last but not least was the proviso that the college would be expected to assess and evaluate components of its program, both for its own benefit and for UCLA's.

Strong academic standards were to be established both for student performance and for the enriched transfer curriculum itself. The TAP or honors program was expected to set specific entrance, maintenance, and completion criteria for its group of general education and/or premajor courses, which the two-year college would guarantee to offer regularly. Most colleges in the first TAP group chose a 3.25 GPA criterion for student membership, and program completion was generally set at fifteen units of UC transferable courses—that is, 25 percent of the 60-unit transfer requirement. The faculty program director would be required to monitor the progress of students and officially certify to UCLA that they had completed the program and were eligible for the priority admission consideration.

One of the original driving forces for TAP had been the need to diversify the student body at UCLA, and there was a strong expectation that culturally and ethnically diverse groups of community college students would be recruited to take advantage of the TAP opportunity. UCLA recommended that an active network of faculty members, students, and counselors be gathered at the college to share information about the program and its activities. There should be an interweaving of UCLA resources (outreach visits by UCLA personnel, student visitation to the university, pretransfer counseling by UCLA staff, articulation documents, and catalogs) with two-year college resources (transfer center, academic and personal counseling offices, financial aid advisers, and so on). Of key importance was the expectation that a particular counselor would be designated to work with individual TAP or honors students throughout their time at the college, and to represent the counseling voice at the quarterly meetings of the TAP council.

UCLA's Responsibilities Within TAP. The level of expectation that UCLA pressed on its community college partners in the first years of TAP had in some cases caused resistance among college leaders, who wondered what they had to gain in return for such extended commitments on their part and such intrusions into their policies and practices by UCLA. It was especially gratifying that when the two-year institutions outspokenly expressed their own high expectations to their prestigious partner, UCLA concurred forthrightly and wholeheartedly. To the many warriors who invested years of intention and energy into its fruition, the word *alliance*—the very center of the TAP acronym, was at last an especially sweet reality.

To oversee TAP, and to provide the incentives sought by their transfer partners, UCLA had designed a triune leadership structure, which enlisted individuals from several offices of undergraduate support services under the overall direction of an academic dean. The College of Letters and Science would provide intersegmental linkages and build student identification with UCLA prior to transfer, facilitate some logistics in the admissions process and advocate for TAP-certified students during the admission cycle, support the UCLA Transfer Student Association in its service to TAP students, and work on special events and privileges that would develop student interest and commitment to the University. Among these privileges were access to library cards and a range of academic, cultural, and sporting events.

The admissions office would be responsible for disseminating information on application procedures and special programs, as well as providing an array of outreach services. Most important, this office would review student applications and determine eligibility for guaranteed priority admission. One of the great successes of TAP from the outset was the extent to which the TAP directors at the two-year colleges were party to detailed discussions, even protracted negotiations, with the UCLA admissions office, concerning the progress of individual students through the transfer application process.

The most significant work in maintaining the multifaceted nature of the collaboration between university and community college was assigned to the UCLA Office of Academic Interinstitutional Programs. Its representative, serving also as a liaison to the UCLA faculty, would work with TAP college administrators, faculty members, and advisory committees to develop and expand their TAP/honors academic enrichment programs. Both longstanding and newly created intersegmental faculty dialogues and academic alliances would be nurtured. Recruitment efforts by the two-year colleges, especially when extended to underrepresented populations at feeder high schools or in community settings, would be linked whenever possible to special UCLA projects and grants. Periodic review of college TAP programs and longitudinal studies of transfer student performance at UCLA would be conducted, and the results would be reinvested in program improvement. The office would organize task forces when appropriate, to work with the colleges to enrich college curriculum, improve teaching methods and strategies, and develop general programs.

Honors Within and Beyond the Transfer Function

For most of the thirty or so two-year colleges who sent representatives to UCLA for a one-day "Build Your Own Honors Program" workshop in December 1995, *honors* had to be defined in the most basic and practical terms. The first program in California had been around for only seven years, and by workshop time only a handful were known among over a hundred colleges throughout the state. The organizers led the participants through the steps of program design that provided both substance and confidence for their work back home. The workshop motto gave them all a battle flag, at once amusing and prophetic: we were joined once and for all in "The Honors Conspiracy."

By May 1986, a dramatically expanded stage, and a better prepared audience, awaited the players. By now there were fifteen community college honors programs in California. Again hosted by UCLA, and sponsored by the University's Office of Academic Interinstitutional Programs and the Western Regional Honors Council, a conjoint conference entitled "2 + 2: The Brightest and the Best" attracted over a hundred two- and four-year institutions from around the United States. The call for papers issued "a challenge to two-year and four-year institutions to provide the best postsecondary experience possible for the broad range of our transfer-oriented and highly motivated students." This time, the agenda stretched over three days, began its first day with a session called "Beginning in Honors," and presented a full palette of sessions on comparative program designs, administrative and political issues, faculty and student recruitment, honors classroom pedagogy, student advisement, and models for extracurricular support.

The closing session was prophetic, and it perfectly culminated several years of systematic work by UCLA and its regional feeder community colleges. It was entitled "Initiating Two-Year/Four-Year Alliances" and was presented by both UCLA and community college representatives. There, in front of the attendees, was a total template for honors in the CCC—from rationale to design to fruition as a principal mode of transfer for students to the University.

Most of the Los Angeles area two-year institutions that took up the UCLA challenge to implement TAP by committing to enrich their transfer preparation curricula for students built the word *honors* directly into their new programs, and duly took their case for support to campus leaders. Surprisingly, responses were mixed and occasionally negative. Honors proponents at a number of campuses had to find ways to tiptoe through delicate diplomatic pathways to assure approval. Because the word *honors* itself seemed to be a lightning rod, several programs were driven to use new titles and acronyms for their programs, to finesse the volatile issues of favoritism or elitism that had proven to be endemic to the development of honors programs across the country (Austin, 1991). One college chose HITE (high-intensity transfer experience), several more used "scholars program," and virtually all construed their program in light of its value in preparing students for transfer.

A serious difficulty faced by many honors proponents was how to address the perception that such programs were inherently elitist because they would serve only a small minority of students. The expectation that enrichment of the curricula for these students would bring more resources and attention their way, and would afford them and their instructors the luxury of smaller class size and extra money and access to college resources, struck many as antithetical to the mission of community colleges. This was worrisome for administrators and general faculty leaders as well, because for them the chronic problem of matching budget deficiencies and the wide range of programs could not be reconciled as it was. Many skeptics brought up the point that if, indeed, honors students were more talented and more motivated, then they were inherently more able to succeed without the extra attention and resources that honors programs seemed to require. And what of the needs of vocational students, part-time students, and reentry students—all part of the student population and all deserving of attention and support? For the community colleges to *fully* implement honors in their own universe, they would have to expand their vision to include vocational or occupational students and faculty members. Following is a description of one of the few comprehensive community college honors programs in the country.

Building a Comprehensive Community College Honors Program

The transfer function mandate for honors would not have been enough to convince administrative, faculty, and student leaders in the San Diego Community College District (SDCCD). Fortunately, at the same time that the historic discussions on academic enrichment/honors/transfer alliances were taking place at UCLA, indeed around the country, the SDCCD was undergoing its own comprehensive self-study—the SUCCESS Project. It was ordered by its publicly elected board of trustees, who gave carte blanche to a number of broadly representative study groups to scrutinize and recommend improvements in every component of district operations.

A faculty-driven subcommittee of the instructional self-study group was commissioned to determine the feasibility of implementing an honors program in the district. An early, and politically prudent, determination was that an honors program must be made available to all qualified students in the district. This brought immediate encouragement from district leadership, because it could be defended as consistent not only with the formal mission statement of the SDCCD, but also with the State of California mandates for instruction in the CCC to provide transfer, occupational, remedial, continuing/adult, and community service programs. Another key insight came from monographs supplied by the National Collegiate Honors Council, which stressed that "there is no one model of an honors program that can be superimposed on . . . institutions nominally of the same sort but different in history, administrative structure, disciplinary organization, budgetary support, or student mix. The basic honors question is: What opportunities must we make available in order to assure that the ablest and/or most highly motivated students in this institution may have their educational needs met?" (Austin, 1991, p. 1). It was an easy step to take in declaring that the goal of the new SDCCD honors program would be to enhance transferability or employability of district students.

Resolving Early Issues of Elitism. Perceptions that an honors program would either demonstrate unwarranted favoritism to a small group of "able and motivated" students and their professors or withhold by default scarce resources from students who were more needy of support are common in the honors literature (Austin, 1991). Not unexpectedly, they were raised by detractors in the SDCCD. The honors steering committee/design group was careful to include in its rationale a set of guidelines that would address head-on the issue of elitism. Program literature included the slogan "Excellence with Access," and it stressed the many ways in which honors experiences were to be made available to students and faculty members. Recruitment initiatives to all area high schools and to all continuing college students would work toward broad ethnic representation and would complement the curriculum vision of enrichment through interdisciplinary and multicultural experiences. Multiple criteria would be adopted for admission to the program, including an ultimate prerogative by an instructor to admit students conditionally by interview.

There were even ways to turn the elitism and favoritism arguments around. In several new and exciting ways, honors would afford to our students the educational opportunities usually reserved for expensive private liberal arts institutions. Once the program was running in the SDCCD and the benefits to both students and faculty members became manifest, expectations and motivation for excellence would spread beyond honors classes to the rest of the curriculum as well, especially as the same students and faculty members were also involved in nonhonors courses. The design group was able to show that although the district's formal commitment was to serve equally the needs of all its students, there was a great disparity in the attention, services, and resources allotted to the remedial student, over the "able and motivated" student. With opposition mollified, at least to the "wait and see" level, the steering committee could concentrate on issues of curriculum design, course selection, and designation of teaching faculty members.

Affording an Honors Program. Again, the timing of the SUCCESS program was propitious. The board of trustees was able to float the nascent SDCCD honors program on State of California lottery funds, with an eye to monitoring the cost to benefit results for a two-year pilot project that would not have to take money away from existing programs. This option turned out to be very important, with support among the leaders of the three colleges uneven, and the districtwide competition for scarce resources always "one short step from frenzy." It was especially gratifying that after only one year of operation, and after a systematic evaluation that led to strong endorsement from the Office of Research and Planning, the board voted to institutionalize the honors program and directed that appropriate resources be supplied.

The SDCCD mandate for honors set up a district honors committee, with faculty and administrative representation from each college, and it bestowed authority to set up policies and procedures for the selection of courses, faculty members, and students. In its first few years, the committee's work was funded from district budget categories. More recently, the instructional components have become imbedded in the operations of the individual campuses, whereas activities common to all campuses—including conference travel, marketing and publications, and faculty-assigned time—remain the responsibility of the district.

The San Diego City College Honors Program. Even as the district honors committee set criteria for the selection each semester of courses at all colleges, via a department-initiated proposal mechanism, each college began to explore its own institutional options for honors offerings. At City College, a landmark decision by the faculty and administrative leadership in the mid-1990s—nearly ten years after the first courses were offered on campus—established a setting aside of funds to guarantee the scheduling of ten honors sections per semester (which, at this writing, is about to be expanded to twelve). Faculty coordinators continued to work hard to ensure that course proposals would come from as many departments as possible, deriving special satisfaction (and general kudos) from the inclusion of courses from constituencies not traditionally served by honors: nursing, cosmetology, business, health science/physical education, manufacturing technology, and computer and information sciences. Furthermore, it was possible to participate in honors courses even if one were a part-time or evening student or professor.

In the past several years, the total number of honors students at City College has increased dramatically. The implicit maximum of just over two hundred students—roughly the agreed-upon capacity of our ten honors sections—has long since been matched by the number of students who have independently initiated honors contracts with their professors. At this writing, contracts provide supplementary honors-level objectives in over ninety courses across the college curriculum and serve more than two hundred additional students.

Launching "The World of Ideas," an Honors General Education Core Curriculum. It would turn out in the long run that the curriculum created to serve transfer students would receive the most attention from stakeholders—both inside and outside the college community. As a set of interconnected courses with thematic linkages, assignment and grading patterns that bridged course boundaries, and extensive collaboration by instructional faculty members, this "core" of classes was an easy conceptual sell to prospective students, faculty curriculum leaders, college and district administrators, and the four-year institutions to whom our students would transfer. "A World of Ideas" was structured around courses that had already been articulated with four-year institutions, and which would soon be fully compatible with the Intersegmental General Education Transfer Curriculum (IGETC) course pattern already approved throughout California by all three systems of higher education. It would serve its design philosophy well: not only would it develop curriculum diversity under the rubrics of interdisciplinary and multicultural/multinational education, but it would also help draw students from diverse populations who could benefit from its possibilities and challenges.

Developing "Our One World," a General Education Honors Curriculum with a Global Theme. The first iterations of the honors general education core had paired first-semester courses in philosophy and English composition, followed by a second-semester pairing of Humanities I and English Composition II/Critical Thinking, and then concluded in the second year with a second humanities course and an open elective from among the other honors-level sections taught collegewide. The current version of the core curriculum, "Our One World," has permuted slightly, leading off with stand-alone cultural anthropology and English Composition I courses, maintaining the second-semester humanities/English pair, and generally offering a more flexible and open selection of courses, including honors contracts, to fill out a completion requirement of fifteen university-transferable units. It is flavored by the work of a two-year, districtwide project that infused key honors courses with a set of student-centered "global competencies." This development reinforces our view that both our honors curricula and the students we send on to four-year institutions should reflect a high level of preparation to contribute in the broadest way to the "global culture in the making."

What Makes Our Honors Courses *Honors*? This question has been unremitting, sometimes abrasively so, over the past fifteen years of the SDCCD program. On one front, the district honors committee has responded with a set of general criteria for course selection, which are employed during the process of proposal review and recommendation. Compared with a nonhonors course on the same content, an honors course must be distinguished by an appropriate combination of its relative rigor, depth, intensity, cross-disciplinary or interdisciplinary character, and/or its innovative teaching/learning modalities. A more extended and detailed response is provided in the document that sets up honors contracts between students and the faculty, which suggests that the inclusion of five or more "honors attributes" distilled from an archive of honors course syllabi would constitute an honors-level experience when added to the objectives of the nonhonors course to which the contract is attached. Presuming comparison with a regular, nonhonors course, the attributes for honors courses include (1) more advanced supplemental reading—especially of primary sources, (2) more opportunities for writing—and at a higher standard, (3) more opportunities for student presentations to class or campus audiences, (4) stronger enhancement of skills in critical thinking, analysis, and interpretation, (5) greater depth and/or breadth of subject matter—especially requiring synthesis of different perspectives or points of view, (6) more opportunities for research—particularly when student-conceived, (7) use of resources or consultants from beyond the campus itself, such as university libraries or interaction with business, academic, or industry personnel, (8) opportunities for publication or public presentation of work, (9) integration of concepts and information from a variety of sources and experiences, particularly in cross- or interdisciplinary contexts, (10) community-based experiences, such as field trips, interviews, and cultural events, and (11) leadership experiences within the class structure, such as leading study groups, leading class discussions, and assisting faculty members in preparation and delivery of instructional material.

Faculty-to-Student Relationships in Honors. From the first moments of the "Build Your Own" honors workshop at UCLA in 1985, it has seemed axiomatic that a close working (and occasionally playing) relationship between a student and a faculty member can illuminate the honors experience for both, and it is a key ingredient in the ultimate success of the student. From an institutional point of view, supporting faculty members in their efforts to recreate curriculum, enrich and broaden their teaching strategies, and open themselves to a more intense and collaborative experience in presenting and discussing their course content is all of major benefit. For those colleges that were close enough to take advantage of the opportunity, the UCLA model of intersegmental "academic alliances" among faculty members in various disciplines (previously described) was especially beneficial in providing a stimulating and confidence-building experience for the college professor—one that gave a pronounced boost to the quality of classroom experiences as well as the commitment to ensure transfer readiness of honors students back home (Banks and Byock, 1991). Students flourished in the interactivity in and away from the honors classroom—with peers, with faculty members, and with other college figures as well (Banks and Byock, 1991). For many students, the intellectual and personal mentoring that accrued in the safe, if demanding, relationship with faculty members was acknowledged as a principal factor in their eventual success, even after transfer. Although not all studies concur (Laanan, 1995, 1996), it has been found that "informally, there was a socializing process within the TAP [UCLA] that suggested [that] the combined effects of the program's curriculum, activities, and interactions with the faculty developed a 'political capacity' within students. This political capacity refers to the student developing an understanding for how academic systems work and a self-confidence in how to manipulate them" (Banks and Byock, 1991, p. 105).

The Role of Extracurricular Experiences in Honors. Students report unfailingly that the most enjoyable aspect of participating in a college honors program is the collaborative work, personal support, and social bonding with their peers. It has become a significant priority in the planning process at City College to include special activities to encourage this end: academic events (for example, a visiting lecturer), cultural events (discount tickets to an Old Globe play, perhaps), and purely social events (mid-term beach party, or impromptu in-class pizza delivery). Levels of trust and willingness to share confidences and future plans are built and sustained, and feelings of isolation and lack of commitment seem to diminish markedly. A gratifying level of interest has developed among honors students to participate in community service and honors societies such as Alpha Gamma Sigma—a California organization, and Phi Theta Kappa—an international two-year college organization. Students enrolled in honors classes (not a requirement for either of the honors societies) launched the Honors Student Council, a new student club meant to serve the honors program goals and activities more closely. With our continuing membership in honors organizations outside San Diego proper, there are occasional opportunities for our students to propose and deliver presentations in professional conference settings. The Honors Transfer Council of California (HTCC)—a forty-member community college consortium—held its first annual conference for student participants at the University of California at Irvine in March 2001, and the Western Regional Honors Council (WRHC) and the National Collegiate Honors Council schedule annual conferences open to student participants.

Summary and Conclusion

Community college honors programs have proliferated in California (indeed, across the country) since the mid-1980s. Although principally concerned with transfer students in most cases, *honors* has emerged on many campuses as a flexible and adaptable component of a comprehensive enrichment strategy that is used to enhance both the transferability and the employability of students. A range of ancillary benefits is easily discerned as well. Among them are faculty development, curriculum innovation, and a markedly higher perception of institutional quality by both prospective and matriculating students, as well as the external community in general. The development of intersegmental honors transfer agreements and alliances, launched with the enthusiastic support of the University of California and California State University segments, has regenerated confidence in the excellence of community colleges as transfer institutions.

References

Austin, C. G. *Honors Programs: Development, Review, and Revitalization.* Radford, Va.: National Collegiate Honors Council, 1991.

Banks, D. L., and Byock, G. "The Effects of the Transfer Alliance Program on Its Colleges, Faculty, and Students." Report to the Ford Foundation by the University of California Los Angeles Center for Academic Interinstitutional Programs, 1991.

Bentley-Baker, K. *Honors in the Two-Year College.* Washington, D.C.: National Council of Instructional Administrators, National Collegiate Honors Council, and Community College Humanities Association, 1983.

Clemons, J., Kane, H. R., and McLeod, R. "Bridging the Community College and University Cultures: Ten Years of a Model Program." *National Honors Report,* 1995, *16*(3), 40–44.

Laanan, F. S. "Making the Transition: An Exploratory Study of Academic Achievement, Involvement, Adjustment, and Satisfaction of Transfer Students at UCLA." Report presented to the dean of the College of Letters and Science, University of California, Los Angeles, 1995. (ED 400 889)

Laanan, F. S. "Making the Transition: Understanding the Adjustment Process of Community College Transfer Students." *Community College Review,* 1996, *23*(4), 69–84.

Piland, W. E., and Gould, K. "Community Colleges and Honors Programs: Are They Mutually Exclusive?" *College Board Review,* Spring 1982.

Wilbur, S. "Understanding the Dynamics of Community College–University Collaboration: A Qualitative Study of a Transfer Admissions Program." Unpublished doctoral dissertation, Department of Education, University of California, Los Angeles, 1996.

HERALD R. KANE is a professor of chemistry and a transfer adviser and honors coordinator at San Diego City College in San Diego, California.

4

This chapter discusses policy issues pertaining to minority transfer students and presents a conceptual model for enhancing and facilitating minority transfers.

Toward a More Perfect Union: Reflecting on Trends and Issues for Enhancing the Academic Performance of Minority Transfer Students

Wynetta Y. Lee

In considering minority presence in higher education, Charles Dickens's reflection in *A Tale of Two Cities* seems applicable—it was the best of times and the worst of times. Higher education has transitioned from a closed, almost secret society only accessible to the sons of elite white families to a scholarly community that is much more reflective of the nation's citizenry. For example, minority presence in enrollment data shows improvement among all racial groups over a twenty-year period (National Center for Education Statistics, 2000).

An educated populace benefits not only individuals but also the local, national, and international levels of community. Research has shown that there is a positive relationship between educational attainment and income earnings (Nettles and Perna, 1997). Higher income earnings enable citizens to be self-reliant contributors to society rather than dependents on public resources. Although there has been progress in the minority attainment of associate's and bachelor's degrees, the progress has been slow, leaving tremendous room for improvement. Successful movement of minorities through the education pipeline from two- to four-year institutions is a strategic means for raising the educational attainment levels of minorities, ultimately improving their income earning potential.

The movement of minorities through the education pipeline from two- to four-year institutions is a phenomenon that merits investigation. A qualitative research paradigm was selected because it is best suited for discovery

NEW DIRECTIONS FOR COMMUNITY COLLEGES, no. 114, Summer 2001   © John Wiley & Sons, Inc.

of the issues that enhance or deter successful transfer between institutions from the transfer student's perspective. The intent was to identify students who successfully transitioned between institutions and to gain an understanding of the recurring themes that could possibly be used to foster the transfer success of other minority students. To that end, qualitative data were collected from minority (African American) students who demonstrated success in movement through the education pipeline. Students were identified through institutional records and were selected for possible inclusion in the study if they successfully completed twelve or more hours at a two-year institution prior to transfer *and* if they had successfully completed twelve or more hours at the four-year institution. These data were collected by using a semi-structured interview protocol to guide the interview sessions. A series of one-hour interview sessions (four focus groups and three individual interviews) were conducted and the sessions involved a total of twelve African American students at a large Research I university in the southeastern United States. Data analysis consisted of content analyses of interview data to determine the recurring themes that emerged from the data. The decision rule for a recurring theme was that it had to emerge in three of the focus groups and two of the individual interview sessions. Therefore, the themes would reflect the consensus of the majority of the students in the sample. The major recurring themes that have emerged from the analysis of the qualitative data indicate that the influences of policy, programs, performance, and people either enhanced or deterred the success of transfer students.

Policy

The general policies regarding transfer are found in articulation agreements between institutions, with an emerging trend of articulation agreements between systems of public higher education. The articulation agreements, under ideal circumstances, are a means of standardizing the transfer process and theoretically should enhance the chances of movement through the educational pipeline. Although the process is specified on paper, the implementation of the process is subject to interpretation by many within both institutions. A policy that is intended to make the process clear and specific is, in effect, a source of confusion and frustration for the students whom it is intended to benefit. One female student described the frustration of the transfer process as "running in quicksand." She went on to report that "when you think you understand the rules, they change, leaving students feeling as though they are moving but sinking fast." The data indicate that the information the students received about the transfer process at the two-year institutions would somehow become either obsolete or inaccurate when they reached the university.

The consequences of the policy knowledge gap between the two- and four-year institutions were clearly articulated by one female student who stated, "It's a scary thing to find out that you are clueless when you are walkin' 'round thinking that you got it all together. It's just by luck that I found out I was going down a dead-end path when I got here. I found out by accident when one of the white girls from my school [community college] just happened to be moaning to me about what she had to take. . . . It's like the rules changed and nobody told me."

The university requires academic advising for students that will keep them accurately informed about institutional policy. However, the data suggested that students are seldom proactive in seeking advice or in confirming the accuracy of their information on a regular basis, which could be a deterrent to their successfully completing their degree. Efforts of institutions to be more intrusive in disseminating transfer policy, especially as requirements change, would likely be an asset to successful college transfer.

Programs

Two-year institutions have specific curricular programs that are identified for students who intend to transfer to four-year institutions. These programs, according to the data, have staff members who are designated to guide students' curricular decisions, identify other student needs, and point them in the right direction for addressing their needs. The two-year institutions the students in the study attended were much smaller in size than the university and much easier to manage. However, students indicated that there is not a specific transfer program at the university that lends the same initial support. The students have advisers available to help them make course selections, but they lack a sense of having a centralized source of information. Although essential information was disseminated through orientation activities, the vast amount of material was too much to absorb for effective use at a later time. In addition, the size of the university and the numerous offices that could only serve specific needs contributed to the students' sense of detachment from the institution. One student indicated that the process of getting information in the university was "like surfing the Internet—if you are persistent you will luck up on what you need to know."

The data indicate that students still occasionally contact faculty and staff members in the two-year institutions for advice and support and that they struggle to find a faculty or staff mentoring relationship in the university similar to that which they experienced in the two-year college. One male student illustrated this point when he stated, "This place is soooo white and I am obviously *not!* I am sure they look at me and see a black man who won't make it here. . . . Nobody has proved me wrong yet. It's better for me to call somebody I already know [to ask questions] back at my old school than it is to ask anybody anything around here 'cause I don't want them [university faculty and staff] to think I'm weak."

Often, minority transfer students rely on other students they know for information and even advice regarding academic planning. This type of peer mentoring is very informal and unstructured. However, the interactions are also unsupervised and the quality of information exchanged is unknown. A more structured mentoring function, especially during the first year of transfer, would benefit students by demystifying the university environment, which would promote a stronger feeling of connection to the institution.

Performance Assessment

Students indicated that they were happy to participate in the study because it was the first time they were asked about their educational experiences and their level of satisfaction with the university. Institutional assessment strategies that focus on this group would not only yield important information about organizational performance—such as how many students are entering and persisting in which fields, but it would also provide a means of helping students feel connected to the institution as a valued asset. One African American female student who planned a major in physical and mathematical sciences illustrated this pattern clearly when she expressed her appreciation for being invited to participate in the study. According to a female student in mathematics:

> This is a very big place and everyone is busy, locked into the pressure of their own worlds. I often wonder if anybody even knows that I am here or if I am simply just another number in the crowd. I have good support from my family and from my friends and it helps me to stay in my right mind. It is easy to go crazy around here if you don't have a rope to hold on to. I just wish that this study was goin' on when I first came here because I would have known that somebody was at least thinking about what I might be going through being black and female in a science and math area.

It was interesting to discover that institutional performance assessments could have a positive effect on both the students' connection to the institution and their sense of identity and value to the institution.

People

Minority students in predominantly white institutions must find ways (positive and some not so positive) to manage their cultural realities within the university environment. Positive management of their cultural realities is dependent on the quality of interaction they have with staff members, however brief that interaction might be. Cultural competence is the extent to which an individual can effectively communicate in cross-cultural situations (Hernandez, Isaacs, Nesman, and Burns, 1998). Cross-cultural communication between minority students and predominant-race faculty and staff members is very likely, given the numbers in each group. Culturally competent faculty and staff members are an important component in helping minority students feel a connection with the university.

Students were asked to discuss their ability to communicate with faculty and staff members belonging to a different race. The emerging themes indicate less than positive circumstances for cross-cultural communications with university personnel. Students were uncomfortable and suspicious during these interactions. One young man illustrated this condition when he indicated that "the [white] people say they want to help but I get the feeling that I'm one great big fat bother. They stare at you when you're talking—looking at you like you're stupid. You can see them wondering how you got in here. The only thing worse is when they talk to you with extra politeness in a really soft voice. It makes you feel small. I always wonder if they are tellin' me right. That stuff stays on my mind when I should be getting work done."

What the student perceived as staring is most likely viewed among institutional staff members as being attentive—a cultural difference in effective communication between races. Clearly, culturally competent staff members who can communicate well in cross-cultural circumstances would enhance students' ability to successfully move toward degree completion in the transfer process.

Concluding Thoughts

It is understandable that research universities cannot embrace a philosophy of being "all things to all people." That mission is being filled by the nation's community colleges. Nonetheless, universities should become more things to more people, given the increasingly diverse populations that are being served.

Clearly stated policies regarding college transfer and articulation policies are beneficial, but ensuring that the respective policies are up to date and widely disseminated at all institutions is crucial to enhancing minority transfer and would probably help majority students.

Moreover, four-year institutions must carefully monitor practices to ensure that all transfer students are treated in an equitable fashion. It is very important for four-year institutions to assess the level of cultural competence that faculty and staff members have for effectively interacting with minority students. Verbal language, tone of voice, and body language are all essential elements in cross-cultural communication that institutional staff members should consider from the students' perspective.

Successful policy and practice will require four-year institutions to make the transition from providing educational and other services in a mass delivery system to accommodating the diversity of its students, including minority students who transfer from two-year institutions that reward teaching to four-year institutions that reward research. This transition is likely to be a major investment on the part of the university. However, the potential reward of minority students' successful movement in the educational pipeline toward degree completion is well worth the investment.

References

Hernandez, M., Isaacs, M. R., Nesman, T., and Burns, D. "Perspectives on Culturally Competent Systems of Care." In M. Hernandez and M. R. Isaacs (eds.), *Promoting Cultural Competence in Children's Mental Health Services*. Baltimore, Md.: Paul H. Brookes, 1998.

National Center for Education Statistics. *Digest of Education Statistics, 2000*. Washington, D.C.: National Center for Education Statistics, U.S. Department of Education, 2000.

Nettles, M. T., and Perna, L. W. *The African American Education Data Book*, Vol. 1: *Higher and Adult Education*. Frederick D. Patterson Research Institute, College Fund/UNCF, 1997.

WYNETTA Y. LEE *is associate professor of higher education in the Department of Adult and Community College Education at North Carolina State University, Raleigh, North Carolina.*

5

This chapter highlights findings from a recent study addressing the issues of students who transfer between community colleges and public universities in the state of Oregon. Implications for policymakers and institutional practitioners are discussed.

Student Transfer Between Oregon Community Colleges and Oregon University System Institutions

James C. Arnold

In 1999, the Oregon Joint Boards of Education (the Board of Higher Education and the Board of Education) accepted and endorsed a report on transfer and articulation that was subsequently presented to the 70th Oregon Legislative Assembly. That document, entitled "A Plan for Course and Credit Transfer Between Oregon Community Colleges and Oregon University System Institutions" (Oregon University System, 1999), had been mandated in HB 2387 (ORS 341.425) as passed by the 69th Legislative Assembly. Concerns about the viability of the student transfer process, especially as it pertained to community college students who wished to transfer to an Oregon University System campus, had led to the legislation and the subsequent joint boards report.

The plan stipulated, and then fully substantiated, two major premises about the student transfer process in Oregon—namely, that (1) course and credit transfer among the public institutions is a successfully completed process in the overwhelming majority of cases, and (2) an effective infrastructure is currently in place to monitor as well as address course and credit transfer issues when they arise. Communication and collaboration efforts between the community colleges and universities—the two major themes of the report—were exhaustively documented to demonstrate the effectiveness of the present system.

One of the concluding elements of the plan, however, called for "ongoing data-collection and research efforts"—in order to continue monitoring

New Directions for Community Colleges, no. 114, Summer 2001 © John Wiley & Sons, Inc.

the course and credit transfer process and to guide future policymaking in this area. A study was recently completed (Arnold, 2000) in response to that recommendation. This chapter presents a summary of that project—a product of four years of data-matching efforts by the Oregon University System (OUS) and the Department of Community Colleges and Workforce Development (CCWD). Implications for policymakers as well as institutional practitioners are also addressed.

Methods and Data Sources

Of course, using such a broad definition of transfer may be viewed as somewhat problematic. Captured in this definition, for example, are students such as (1) "reverse transfers" (university students who may enroll for a community college course during the summer term), coenrolled students (students simultaneously enrolled in a community college and a university), and graduate students (who may, for example, enroll in a community college for personal enrichment or employment-enhancing experiences). However, sorting these students out has not yet been possible (or attempted) using the data-matching methods employed for this study. This broadened definition of transfer student should be kept in mind when viewing the data presented here.

The data used in this study, presented to assess the status of transfer student activity and performance in the state of Oregon, are now regularly collected by OUS and CCWD. Each year since 1995–96, the staff of OUS and CCWD have collaborated in a data-match project whereby the social security numbers (SSNs) of all community college and public university students are compared. Information about students who were community college students one year and then were enrolled at an OUS institution the next academic year may be extracted by matching these SSNs. In comparing records from the two sectors in this manner, the definition of *transfer student* is greatly expanded over the individual OUS institutional definitions, which define transfer students as those *admitted* students who have presented a minimum number of hours of college-level work as evidence of eligibility for admission. Using these data, it is possible to obtain a broader picture of the scope of transfer activity, as well as to better gauge the performance of students, once they make the transition from community college- to university-level work.

Results

Data from each of the last four years are summarized in the following tables. Not all data elements are available for all four years of the data-match project, however. The ability of community colleges to synthesize and forward their data to CCWD improves each year, as does the expertise of the OUS and CCWD personnel charged with sorting and matching the data. Every year of the data-match effort, the reliability of these data is believed to increase.

All Oregon Community College Students Transferring to an Oregon University System Institution: Total Number and Proportion by Gender, Race, and Residency Status. The number of students who were enrolled at an Oregon community college one year and then enrolled at an Oregon University System institution the next year are listed year by year and summarized in Table 5.1. The "Academic Year" column indicates the year students enrolled in OUS—that is, on any campus for any course. Those students had attended an Oregon community college the previous year—that is, any campus, any level of activity. For each of the four years included in this study, the total number of students "transferring" is listed in the "All Transfers" column and is compared with the total number of "Admitted Transfers" for the academic year. The figures are unduplicated counts of all students at all levels.

For 1998–99, the racial and ethnic distribution of all Oregon community college transfer students is presented in Table 5.2. In an unduplicated count for 1998–99, other characteristics of "all transfer" students include the following: 54 percent were female and 46 percent were male; 95 percent were Oregon residents and 5 percent were nonresidents (for fee purposes). Furthermore, 4,244 students were transfer students from sources other than Oregon community colleges. Of these, 1,274 were from other Oregon colleges and universities and 1,958 were from out of state, with 1,012 having unknown origins. These 4,244 students who transferred into an OUS institution represented a total of at least 426 campuses from around the world.

Summary. Overall transfer student activity from year to year is quite stable in Oregon; the number of admitted transfer students and "all transfers" has risen modestly between 1996–97 and 1998–99. A majority (54 percent) of transfer students are female, and the overwhelming majority (95 percent) of the Oregon community college-to-OUS transfer population are Oregon residents for fee purposes. OUS institutions generally attract transfer students of color from the community colleges in at least the same proportion in which they are represented on the two-year campuses. In addition to attracting Oregon community college transfers, OUS also attracts a large number of other transfer students, both from within Oregon and from outside the state.

Table 5.1. Comparison of "All Transfers" (from Oregon Community Colleges to Oregon University System Institutions) per Academic Year with "Admitted Transfers"

Academic Year	All Transfers	Admitted Transfers
1995–96	10,359	3,330
1996–97	10,255	3,158
1997–98	10,280	3,327
1998–99	11,595	3,687

Oregon Community College Students Completing an Associate of
Arts/Oregon Transfer (AA/OT) Degree: Total Number, Proportion, and
Average Credits Transferred, and Lower-Division Collegiate Students
Transferring. For the four years of the data-match project, Table 5.3 lists
the numbers of associate of arts/Oregon transfer (AA/OT) degree-bearing
students who have appeared on OUS campuses the following year (as well
as the percentages of all AA/OT degrees awarded the previous year). The
average number of quarter credits accepted by OUS institutions upon transfer are available for two of the years of this project. Both the number and
proportion of transfer degree students have remained stable, as well as the
number of credits transferred, which is slightly above the minimum number required (ninety) for the AA/OT degree itself. (Note: Students who
transfer to an OUS institution with an AA/OT have fulfilled all the lower-
division general education requirements of the receiving institution and are
permitted to register as juniors.)

**Table 5.2. Comparison of Race/Ethnicity of All 1998–99 Transfer
Students (from Oregon Community College to Oregon University
System Institution) with All Community College Students
and All OUS Students**

Race/Ethnicity	1998–99 Transfer Students	1997–98 All OR CC Students	1998–99 All OUS Students
Asian	7.1%	2.8%	6.1%
Black	1.3%	1.3%	1.5%
Caucasian	74.6%	63.4%	73.0%
Hispanic	3.3%	5.3%	3.1%
Native American	1.4%	1.4%	1.3%
International	1.9%	2.0%	5.8%
Unknown	10.3%	23.8%	9.1%
Total	100.0%	100.0%	100.0%

**Table 5.3. Number of Students Completing an Oregon Transfer
Degree One Year and Then Enrolling in an Oregon University System
Institution the Next Academic Year**

Academic Year	AA/OTs Transferring In	% of All AA/OTs	Average Credits Transferred In
1995–96	895	48%	Not available
1996–97	1,101	56%	98
1997–98	1,015	55%	99
1998–99	1,037	54%	Not available

Most Oregon community college students transfer to an OUS institution *without* having completed a community college degree. In fact (see also Table 5.1), the total number of AA/OT transfers is about 10 percent of "all transfers" and less than one-third of "admitted transfers." The total number of students who were enrolled in a lower-division collegiate course or program is reflected in Table 5.4. Lower-division collegiate students are those who have a declared major, indicating their intent to eventually transfer to a baccalaureate-granting institution.

Summary. These data indicate that the number of students having completed the AA/OT who transfer to OUS is essentially stable and represents approximately 55 percent of all students who earn the baccalaureate degree in any given year. The percentage of students enrolled in a lower-division collegiate program for any year, and who then transfer, is also essentially stable, although they transfer at a lower rate than those students having earned a transfer degree. The number of AA/OT graduates who appear on an OUS campus in a year other than the one immediately following their degree is unknown, although the assumption is that more of these students do eventually appear.

Oregon Community College Students Transferring to an Oregon University System Institution: Academic Performance After Transfer. Many first-time freshmen, transfer students, and other continuing students are in need of remedial coursework at some point. Table 5.5 outlines the total number of Oregon community college students who enroll in remedial mathematics courses during their first year at an OUS institution. Remedial mathematics is defined, for the purposes of this study, as any math course with a number below 100. Data such as these are important for estimating the level of preparation and eventual success of students who pursue a bachelor's degree. Adelman (1999, p. vii) has found that the highest level of math studied in high school has "the strongest continuing influence on bachelor's degree attainment." That is, completing a high school course beyond second-year algebra more than doubles the chance that a student will ultimately complete a baccalaureate degree.

Of the 4,244 undergraduate students attending an OUS institution in the "other transfer" category for 1998–99 (all transfer students whose last institution attended was other than an Oregon community college or who

Table 5.4. Number of Lower-Division Collegiate (LDC) Students Enrolled at an Oregon Community College One Year and Then Enrolling in an Oregon University System Institution the Next Academic Year

Academic Year	LDC Transfer Students	Total LDC Students	% of LDC Students Transferring
1997–98	7,767	54,895	14%
1998–99	8,202	57,415	14%

Table 5.5. Oregon Community College Students Taking Remedial Mathematics After Transfer to an OUS Institution

Academic Year	All Undergraduate Transfers (Unduplicated)	Number Taking Remedial Mathematics	% Taking Remedial Mathematics
1996–97	6,691	46	0.7%
1997–98	8,231	65	0.8%
1998–99	9,098	82	0.9%

Table 5.6. Academic Performance of All Oregon Community College Transfer Students in All Oregon University System Courses

Academic Year	All Undergraduate Transfers (Unduplicated)	GPA for All Courses
1996–97	7,546	2.91
1997–98	8,062	2.92
1998–99	8,865	2.94

had attended an Oregon community college in another year), fifty-three of them (1.2 percent) enrolled in remedial mathematics during the year.

Turning to the performance of Oregon community college students in their primary academic courses after transfer, Table 5.6 lists, for three of the years of the data-match project, the overall grade point average (GPA) for all transfer students enrolled in graded courses. By way of comparison, the 4,070 students attending an OUS institution in the "other transfer" category for 1998–99 (all transfer students whose last institution attended was other than an Oregon community college or who had attended an Oregon community college in another year) earned an overall GPA of 3.06, and the 6,988 first-time freshmen earned an overall GPA of 2.80.

In terms of academic performance of Oregon community college transfer students in a specific disciplinary area, Table 5.7 presents two years of GPA data for those enrolled in OUS math courses. By way of comparison, Table 5.8 lists the performance of first-time freshmen as well as other transfer students in the same courses (for the 1998–99 academic year only).

In addition, Table 5.9 illustrates the academic performance of Oregon community college students in a variety of disciplinary areas for two academic years. "Arts and letters" includes such areas as art, communication, English, journalism, music, humanities, philosophy, and theater. "Sciences" includes such areas as biology, chemistry, physics, astronomy, engineering, and geology. "Social sciences" includes such areas as anthropology, geography, history, political science, psychology, and sociology. "English composition" includes all college-level writing courses. By way of comparison, Table

Table 5.7. Academic Performance of Oregon Community College Transfer Students in Math Courses

Math Course	1997–98 Transfer Students Enrolled	GPA	1998–99 Transfer Students Enrolled	GPA
College algebra	1,032	2.37	1,204	2.50
Precalculus	943	2.37	1,018	2.35
Calculus	654	2.49	733	2.55
Math beyond calculus	348	2.72	427	2.64
All math courses	2,608	2.48	2,941	2.50

Table 5.8. Academic Performance of First-Time Freshmen and Other Transfer Students in Math Courses

Math Course	1998–99 First-Time Freshmen	GPA	1998–99 Other Transfer Students	GPA
College algebra	2,460	2.35	514	2.68
Precalculus	1,559	2.62	441	2.64
Calculus	1,063	2.75	304	2.67
Math beyond calculus	261	2.80	143	2.71
All math courses	4,152	2.51	1,234	2.68

5.10 lists the performance of first-time freshmen as well as other transfer students in the same disciplines (for the 1998–99 academic year only).

Summary. The data pertaining to the performance of transfer students presented in Tables 5.5 to 5.10 have been considerable. Based on the findings, the observations that follow appear to be reasonable. The number of transfer students taking remedial mathematics the first year at their OUS campus is very small, totaling less that 1 percent of all transfer students. The aggregate performance of all community college transfer students in all of their OUS courses during the first year after transfer demonstrates an overall GPA greater than 2.90. This compares favorably with first-time freshmen, who, overall, exhibit an average GPA of 2.80, as well as with other transfer students, who earn an average GPA of 3.06 (1998–99 data). The data for mathematics courses show that community college transfer students perform acceptably. In 1998–99, for college algebra courses, community college transfers (2.50) outperformed first-time freshmen (2.35) but did less well than other transfer students (2.68). In precalculus, calculus, and math beyond calculus, community college transfers did slightly less well than first-time freshmen or other transfers. In looking at *all* math courses, community college transfers (2.50) performed at the same level as first-time

Table 5.9. Academic Performance of Oregon Community College Students in Various Disciplinary Areas

Disciplinary Area	1997–98 Transfer Students Enrolled	GPA	1998–99 Transfer Students Enrolled	GPA
Arts and letters	4,342	3.01	4,702	3.03
Sciences	4,267	2.69	4,553	2.72
Social sciences	5,301	2.88	5,766	2.90
Foreign languages	966	3.05	1,047	3.07
English composition	1,278	3.05	1,333	3.10

Table 5.10. Academic Performance of First-Time Freshmen and Other Transfer Students in Various Disciplinary Areas

Disciplinary Area	1998–99 First-Time Freshmen	GPA	1998–99 Other Transfer Students	GPA
Arts and letters	4,937	2.88	2,295	3.16
Sciences	4,803	2.59	1,893	2.84
Social sciences	5,198	2.59	2,561	3.00
Foreign languages	1,185	3.12	512	3.25
English composition	4,054	3.02	699	3.30

freshmen (2.51), but not quite as well as other transfers (2.68). In a variety of other broad disciplinary areas, community college transfer students also performed well. In 1998–99, in the "arts and letters," "sciences," "social sciences," and "English composition" areas, community college transfer students had overall GPAs that were better than those of first-time freshmen and slightly lower than those of other transfers. In "foreign languages," community college transfer students (3.07) placed about the same as first-time freshmen (3.12) but behind other transfers (3.25).

Retention and Graduation of Oregon Community College Transfer Students at Oregon University System Institutions. Although not specifically a part of the data-match project, the data presented in this section are significant in completing the overall picture of the transfer process in the state of Oregon. The rate at which transfer students persist in their pursuit of the baccalaureate, as well as the rate at which they graduate, has historically been of great interest to all who are involved in decisions and policy-making regarding community college transfer students. Data illuminating these issues follow; data regarding native OUS first-time freshmen are also included for comparison.

At the outset, however, it might be appropriate to note that presenting and examining data of this nature are based on rather outdated notions regarding student enrollment patterns. The concept of "linear transfer,"

Table 5.11. Retention and Graduation of Community College Transfer Students: 1993–94 Cohort, Four Years After Entry (1997)

Status	Number of Students	Percentage of Total
Continuing	203	7.9%
Graduated	1,626	63.1%
Stopped out	747	29.0%
Total	2,576	100.0%

Table 5.12. Retention and Graduation of First-Time Freshmen: 1993–94 Cohort, Six Years After Entry (1999)

Status	Number of Students	Percentage of Total
Continuing	365	5.4%
Graduated	3,554	52.8%
Stopped out	2,813	41.8%
Total	6,732	100.0%

whereby students are viewed as going from high school to community college and then on to a four-year institution, in a linear fashion, and seeking a degree in a timeline that has been thought "traditional" (in four, five, or six years) has been demonstrated to be a part of higher education mythology (Kinnick and others, 1998)—at least in terms of student behavior in the 1990s. When viewing data that are presented in such a way as to suggest that students *should* persist in their educational pursuits continuously, and then graduate in a "timely" fashion, the warning should be issued that students do not necessarily think or behave in these ways. Students today move in and out of attending college, they move between and among the institutions in the entire postsecondary sector, and they may have goals in mind that do not necessarily make a six-year graduation rate a meaningful statistic.

Given the caveats previously mentioned, however, retention and graduation data follow. Table 5.11 presents systemwide data for Oregon community college transfer students four years after their entry into OUS. Table 5.12 then presents systemwide data for native OUS first-time freshmen, six years after entry. These data are presented as merely a starting point for analysis, however. It is difficult to determine the most appropriate manner in which to make transfer student versus native student comparisons. In Table 5.11, transfer students in this entering cohort come to OUS with a variety of experiences—from having the minimum number of credits to qualify as an admitted transfer student to entering OUS with an associate's degree. Is it legitimate to compare this group four years after entry with all first-time freshmen six years after entry? Probably not. However, if allowed to make this comparison, transfer students appear to fare quite well in their university experiences: 63.1 percent have graduated in four years, compared with 52.8 percent of first-time freshmen in six years' time.

A more reasonable and informative manner in which to look at graduation data for these groups might come from a comparison of first-time freshmen who were able to persist through their first year and transfer students who enter OUS with a year or more (45 to 89 quarter credit hours in the group chosen here) of college credits earned at a community college. These data are presented in Table 5.13 for two different cohorts of native OUS students and Oregon community college transfers, six years after entry. In this comparison, community college transfers graduate at the rate of about 62 percent and native OUS freshmen graduate in the 65–68 percentage range.

These data are not inconsistent with findings presented for community college students in the Portland metropolitan area (Kinnick and others, 1998), which demonstrate that for those students transferring to Portland State University from a metro-area community college with an associate of arts/Oregon transfer degree, 67 percent completed their baccalaureate degree. The results for Oregon, though, may be somewhat behind the trend that has been demonstrated nationally. Adelman (1998) has found that, overall—on the basis of an examination of the national longitudinal data from the "High School and Beyond/Sophomore Cohort" (covering the period from 1980 through 1993)—67 percent of students who enrolled in a two- or four-year college directly from high school and attended a four-year college sometime earned a bachelor's degree. Of those students who earned 60-plus semester credits (the equivalent of 90-plus quarter credits or a two-year associate's degree) and attended a four-year college sometime, 79 percent earned a bachelor's degree.

Summary. These data tend to make certain assumptions about student behavior that may or may not be valid. Students today flow freely between and among institutions and pursue their academic goals in such ways that do not necessarily make these graduation rates meaningful statistics. The graduation rates of community college transfer students and those of native students compare quite favorably, however. Transfer students with at least

Table 5.13. Comparison of Six-Year Graduation Rates of OUS First-Time Freshmen Who Persisted Through First Year and Oregon Community College Transfer Students Who Transferred with 45–89 Credit Hours

Entering Cohort	Graduation Rate of First-Time Freshmen (completing one year at OUS)	Graduation Rate of Community College Transfers (with 45–89 transferable hours)
88–89	65.2%	61.9%
93–94	67.6%	62.0%

one year's worth of academic credit have a six-year graduation rate of about 62 percent, whereas native students who persist through their first year have a six-year graduation rate of about 65–68 percent.

Discussion and Policy Implications

Taken together, the Oregon-specific match data pertaining to transfer students, along with the persistence and graduation data, provide a comprehensive look at the phenomenon of student transfer in Oregon. This section is devoted to providing a thoughtful examination of this information.

Transfer Rates and Enrollment Patterns. From enrollment management as well as broader policy perspectives, the number of community college students transferring to four-year campuses is a matter of great interest to institutions on both sides of the transfer divide. Many agreements and programs (in Oregon and elsewhere) have been developed in recent years to facilitate the transition for students, not only with good intentions in mind to ease any possible "transfer shock" (Hills, 1965) that students might experience, but also with an anticipated outcome of increasing the enrollments of transfer students. However, as much of the research has shown, and Oregon figures bear out, the numbers of transfer students from community colleges to baccalaureate institutions are not experiencing much growth. Questions that naturally come to mind include: Why is this so? Should we be doing better? What would "doing better" mean?

Unfortunately, furnishing answers to these questions is highly problematic. Researchers (for example, see Grubb, 1991) who study the transfer process on a national level are able only to speculate on the reasons for "the declining transfer rate." If Oregon should be doing better with numbers of transfer students, that leads to the question: Better than what (or whom)? Data from the neighboring states of Washington and California, for example, indicate that these states have experienced a period of at least five years of stagnant or declining numbers of transfer students entering the public baccalaureate-granting institutions from the community colleges.

In terms of transfer rates in Oregon, this study has examined the number of students entering an OUS institution the year after earning an AA/OT degree. These data indicate that slightly over 50 percent of AA/OT recipients enroll at OUS campuses the year following their degree. Is this a reasonable fraction, given that, a priori, one might suspect that earning a transfer degree signals a student's transfer intent? Again, this is a difficult question to answer, and further investigation is required to place this percentage in a larger context. For example, if one tracks a particular cohort of AA/OT recipients out further than the one-year time period reported here, will data indicate that more of these transfer degree recipients actually appear at an OUS campus? And even more difficult to determine, what is the proportion of AA/OT recipients who ultimately enroll in a private or out-of-state institution?

Research on the topics of student enrollment patterns and choices, nationally and in the state of Oregon (de los Santos and Wright, 1990; Kinnick and others, 1998), suggests that students today do not necessarily attend high school, community college, and a four-year campus in a linear fashion. Students often enroll in more than one institution at a time, transfer back and forth between campuses, and take courses when and where they are most conveniently available to them.

Consequently, in Oregon, to accommodate the needs of students who desire to combine community college and four-year campus coursework in pursuing a baccalaureate degree, many partnership agreements and dual-enrollment/co-admissions programs have been implemented. Programs such as these have been little studied, though, and more recent and reliable data are needed to track the trends, successes, and limitations of such entities.

Given these considerations, then, the following recommendations are offered for policymakers in Oregon:

- Follow-up on students in Oregon who earn the associate of arts/Oregon transfer degree should be enhanced to include tracking of these students more than one year past their degree (and possibly gathering information about those students who choose not to attend a four-year institution, to see how their degrees are being used).
- Data-collection efforts on students simultaneously enrolled in two- and four-year campuses should be expanded. These students are so enrolled as part of official programs as well as by individual student choice. Not enough is known about these students at this time to make well-informed policy decisions.
- Data-collection efforts should be expanded to include follow-ups on students, focusing on the academic major they pursued after transfer. The academic programs in which transfer students enroll may be able to inform curricular decisions at the campus level in both sectors.

Credit Transfer (Acceptance and Loss). Credit acceptance remains a prime concern in any discussion of transfer students. Students frequently lament that credits earned were lost in the transition. Information from the data-match effort shows that students transferring with an AA/OT degree bring about 98–99 credits to their OUS campus, which is slightly over the 90-credit minimum for the degree. These credits transfer in as a block, meaning that all the credits earned for the associate's degree are accepted and transcripted at the four-year level. Even for these students, though, there is the perception of credit loss, as not all of the credits earned always apply to specific major, minor, or other requirements. It is often important, therefore, to remind students that regardless of the amount of work they transfer in, requirements for the baccalaureate must still be met.

Of course, students need not complete a transfer degree before enrolling in a four-year institution. A study of student transcripts in the

Portland metropolitan area (Kinnick and others, 1998) found that the average number of community college credits earned by transfer students was 91, of which, on average, 76 were accepted for transfer, leading to suggestions of credit loss. This study also led to a classification of the reasons earned community college credits were not accepted, including:

- *Low grade:* transfer courses in which students had earned unacceptable grades
- *Developmental education course:* credits earned in non-college-level courses
- *Professional-technical course:* credits earned in professional-technical areas that were not designed for transfer to a four-year institution
- *Duplicate course:* credits appearing on the transcript but which were taken more than once
- *Over maximum allowed:* credits earned beyond the 108 quarter credits that institutional policy allows for transfer

Given the number of legitimate reasons, then, that a student's credits may not apply as anticipated, a much more realistic way to look at this issue is "simply the fact that non-transferable credits were submitted to the university" (Bach and others, 1999, p. 4).

Still, institutions do bear some responsibility, along with their students, to ensure the best use of time and resources, which certainly could include trying to maximize the number of credits accepted. Of critical importance in this process is the role of the adviser, whether that be a faculty member, counselor, or designated individual in an advising office. Staff members charged with dispensing advice to students interested in the transfer process must avail themselves of the most up-to-date information concerning the various options students may wish to pursue, including the transfer degree, dual enrollment programs, articulation agreements for specific programs, and informal arrangements between two- and four-year campuses designed to benefit students who transfer. Students and advisers alike must be sure that they are fully informed about the requirements that need to be fulfilled in order to earn a baccalaureate degree.

Hence, efforts already underway on many campuses should be continued to expand advising information and services available to students with the development and implementation of electronic advising centers. The more information readily available to students, the better they can be served and the better the decisions they will make.

Student Performance. The transfer shock (Hills, 1965) phenomenon is much discussed when addressing the performance of community college transfer students upon their arrival at a four-year campus. There is considerable evidence (Diaz, 1992) to support, as well as refute, the transfer shock notion that the grade point averages of students decline soon after transfer. The data presented in this chapter do not speak precisely to the notion of transfer shock, as no comparisons are made between student performance before transfer and that after transfer. However, the data clearly demonstrate a quite acceptable level of student performance for Oregon community college students who enroll in an OUS institution.

Given the picture provided by these data, then, a reasonable inference is that there is not much of a difference in academic ability between the Oregon community college students and native Oregon University System students who pursue the baccalaureate. Given the overall academic performance of community college students, it would not be unreasonable to conclude that if transfer shock is present for these students, a recovery is likely to be made within the first year (for a result that might be expected, based on other studies, see Diaz, 1992). Oregon community college students appear to be ready for the academic expectations placed on them when they arrive at the four-year campus of their choice, effectively dispelling the myth of inadequate transfer student preparation. Those students who transfer, and have the goal of the baccalaureate in mind, are successful at Oregon University System campuses.

While the aggregated match data are quite useful in presenting the previous analysis, there is at least one limitation of these data: no information about the performance of individual students is available to community colleges that may wish to track student success at that level. This has been a frustration expressed by community college advisers, faculty members, and administrators, even though privacy concerns prohibit such individual student tracking through the use of these data. It is this limitation, however, that gives rise to the recommendation that Oregon University System and Oregon community college administrators and data experts explore (or develop) the legal and ethical means by which to exchange unit-record data so that the success of individual students and small cohorts may be tracked and reported.

Persistence and Graduation.   The questions of how well transfer students persist toward, and ultimately graduate with, a baccalaureate degree are important, especially in terms of comparing the experience of transfer students with that of students native to the four-year campus. Recall, however, that certain caveats were discussed earlier in this chapter in terms of interpreting the available data. For example, the traditional notions of linear transfer and a four- to six-year time to degree appear to be outdated. Students do not necessarily behave consistently with postsecondary education's time-worn data collection and interpretation practices that suggest that today's students act as liberal arts college students did, say, in the fifties, sixties, or seventies. Given all the reservations expressed with regard to these data, though, comparisons have still been made. For community college students entering OUS with 45 to 89 credit hours in transfer work, the six-year graduation rate is about 62 percent. This compares with a six-year graduation rate of 65 to 68 percent for native OUS students who persisted through their first year.

Conclusion

This chapter has summarized a recent study conducted for the Oregon Joint Boards of Education. The data presented originate with the Oregon data-match project, which is a cooperative venture of the Oregon University System and the Department of Community Colleges and Workforce Development. Although initiated in 1995–96, the project is still in its infancy. OUS and CCWD have plans to ensure that the data-collection efforts reported here will be continued, as well as expanded, in order for policymakers in Oregon to make more informed decisions in the areas of articulation and transfer. Policymakers, administrators, faculty members, advisers, and students should be encouraged by the information gathered thus far, however. Transfer activity in the state of Oregon appears to be stable or on the rise, and the academic performance and graduation rate of community college transfer students are at about the same level as those for students who began their postsecondary academic careers at a university.

References

Adelman, C. "What Proportion of College Students Earn a Degree?" *AAHE Bulletin,* Oct. 1998, pp. 7–9.

Adelman, C. *Answers in the Tool Box: Academic Intensity, Attendance Patterns, and Bachelor's Degree Attainment.* Washington, D.C.: Office of Educational Research and Improvement, U.S. Department of Education, 1999.

Arnold, J. C. *Students Who Transfer Between Oregon Community Colleges and Oregon University System Institutions: What the Data Say.* Report submitted to the Joint Boards of Education by the Joint Boards Articulation Commission. Eugene: Oregon University System, 2000.

Bach, S. K., and others. "Case Studies in Transfer Attendance Within an Urban Postsecondary Environment." Paper presented at the 39th annual forum of the Association of Institutional Research, Seattle, 1999.

de los Santos, A. G., Jr., and Wright, I. "Maricopa's Swirling Students." *Community, Technical, and Junior College Journal,* 1990, *60*(6), 32–34.

Diaz, P. E. "Effects of Transfer on Academic Performance of Community College Students at the Four-Year Institution." *Community/Junior College Quarterly,* 1992, *16,* 279–291.

Grubb, W. N. "The Decline of Community College Transfer Rates." *Journal of Higher Education,* 1991, *62,* 194–222.

Hills, J. R. "Transfer Shock: The Academic Performance of the Junior College Transfer." *Journal of Experimental Education,* 1965, *33,* 201–215.

Kinnick, M. K., and others. "Student Transfer Between Community Colleges and a University in an Urban Environment." *Journal of Applied Research in the Community College,* 1998, *5,* 89–99.

Oregon University System. *A Plan for Course and Credit Transfer Between Oregon Community Colleges and Oregon University System Institutions.* Eugene: Oregon University System, 1999.

JAMES C. ARNOLD *is director of community college articulation and policy associate in the office of the chancellor for the Oregon University System in Eugene.*

6

This chapter discusses the different methodological perspectives of the research done on transfer students. Documents from the ERIC database and journal articles are used to answer the questions, Who is conducting research? What methods are being used to gather information? and What types of data are being collected on transfer students? Finally, this chapter presents examples of studies that have implications for researchers and other stakeholders and can be adapted at the institutional level.

Studying Transfer Students: Designs and Methodological Challenges

Carol A. Kozeracki

Each year, thousands of students transfer from a community college to a four-year college or university. Because of the large number of students involved in this process, many individuals and organizations—including administrators, researchers, faculty members, and policymakers—are interested in the progress and academic achievement of these students. A substantial amount of information, usually collected by institutions for purposes other than research, is available to provide the basic facts about the progress of transfer students: how many students transfer, what their grades are at the two- and four-year institutions, and whether they attain a baccalaureate degree. What is less readily available are data that examine the factors that affect student success and that explore the effectiveness of community colleges in preparing students to transfer.

Using documents from the ERIC database and articles from relevant journals, this chapter examines from a methodological perspective the research being done on transfer students—namely, who is conducting the research, what methods are being used to gather the information, and what types of data are being collected. It will also present examples of comprehensive and useful studies that researchers interested in community colleges may want to consider adapting for their own institutions. The purpose of providing these examples is to identify research questions that have been asked and exemplary college programs and practices in place that can be considered by other community colleges to improve the transfer readiness of their students.

The Researchers

Not surprisingly, many of the documents addressing this topic are written by the institutional researchers at community colleges. Reporting requirements in many states mandate that information about student achievement, including degrees and certificates awarded, the number of students transferring, grade point average (GPA), and demographic characteristics—especially related to race and gender—be captured. Thus, the annual reports produced by these offices almost always include some information related to transfer (Arnold and Ugale, 1996; Boughan, 1995). Although these analyses are often based on existing data from the admissions or registrars' offices, sometimes the institutional research offices at these colleges will survey students or graduates to ascertain such things as motivation, aspirations, and satisfaction (Alexander, 1996; Duckwall, 1997; Grosset, 1996; *Kent Trumbull Student Transfer Behavior,* 1995; *Graduate Survey, 1992–93,* 1995). In addition, some institutional researchers have assessed the effectiveness of particular programs, such as honors programs, in improving transfer rates (Lucas, Hull, and Brantley, 1995) or the effectiveness of particular classes in preparing students for the four-year institution (Hoyt, 1999). At one office of research and development, a transfer eligibility measure was developed to complement the college's transfer rate (Rasor and Barr, 1995).

Another common source of information on transfer are the statewide reports that provide overall statistics related to transfer for all the state's community colleges and, sometimes, the entire state's public system of higher education. In most cases, these reports consist almost exclusively of tables and charts presenting the information collected from individual colleges and the totals derived from these data, with little commentary or analysis (Articulation Accountability Committee, 1998; North Carolina Community College System, 1995; State Board of Directors for Community Colleges of Arizona, 1999; Illinois Community College Board, 1998; Walters and Shymoniak, 1996).

University-based researchers also contribute to the literature on student transfer. In some cases, the institutional researchers perform a function similar to that of their community college counterparts: using existing institutional data to analyze the academic performance of transfer students at their university, often in comparison with that of native students (*Community College Transfer Performance at JMU,* 1998). In addition, university professors, usually from the education department, conduct research that may be based at their university or they may look at the performance of students across a state or across the country. Such reports tend to be driven by a specific research question—such as, What affects the transfer rate of African American students? (Blau, 1999), What is the appropriate admissions standard for transfer students? (Saupe and Long, 1996), and Does transfer student performance vary by academic division? (Cejda, 1997).

A limited number of studies on transfer students have been conducted jointly by representatives from community colleges and four-year institutions. One of these studies attempted to identify transfer students' academic difficulties in specific courses at the university (Quanty, Dixon, and Ridley, 1996). Two partnership efforts—one in Washington (Kinnick and others, 1997) and one in Michigan (Adams, 1999)—united universities and community colleges in examining institutional data from the two- and four-year institutions to define the transfer process among and between the institutions. It should be mentioned that Kinnick and others (1997) reported that the data collection and recording phase of the study "was by far the most challenging because of the complexity and volume of the data, differences among institutions in how transcript data were presented, and the form in which transcript evaluation information was available" (p. 92). Conducting research that involves the cooperation of multiple institutions complicates the research process and can lengthen the time for completion, but it can also increase the value of the data.

Two other groups—graduate students (usually in the form of dissertations) and the federal government—also examine and report on transfer students. Dissertations are similar to the studies done by university professors in that they often involve multiple institutions and respond to particular research questions rather than provide descriptive data (Laanan, 1996; Minear, 1998). Several reports have been published by the U.S. Department of Education, using data collected from the 1990 Beginning Postsecondary Student Longitudinal Study, which examines student progress and the relation between intent and achievement (McCormick and Carroll, 1997; U.S. Department of Education, 1997). Clifford Adelman's work (1999), which uses data from the High School and Beyond national data set, has much to say about the impact of transfer and multiple institution attendance on academic achievement.

The Methods

Studies about transfer students use both quantitative and qualitative methodologies. The overwhelming majority of the studies reported in the ERIC database are quantitative—using either existing data gathered by the institution or survey information collected by the researcher. Using existing data is popular because it takes advantage of reliable data that have been collected for other reasons and does not require the cooperation of students, college faculty members, or administrators to complete the study. The types of existing data available are fairly extensive: race, gender, age, full-time/part-time status, course completions, credits earned and transferred, time between high school graduation and college entry, enrollment in developmental courses, retention rates, GPA, SAT scores, and whether the student earned an associate's degree (Arnold and Ugale, 1996; Boughan, 1998; Carlan and Byxbe,

2000; Lanni, 1997; Minear, 1998; Rice, 1996). These studies have emanated from both the community colleges and the universities, and tend to focus on student progress at one institution (either the community college or the four-year institution). Many of the studies are descriptive, whereas others use more sophisticated techniques. One study used regression analysis in an attempt to predict transfer student academic success, finding that lower-division GPA and college major were significant predictors (Carlan and Byxbe, 2000). Another study of African American students used logistic regression to predict the factors that contribute to nonsuccess: English assessment, full-time/part-time status, math assessment, gender, and work hours (Lanni, 1997). One other study, conducted by a community college institutional researcher, used path and cluster analyses to predict academic success for students at one community college. The researcher found that personal motivation (inferred from other factors), student participation in institutional support services, and a structured accumulation of academic difficulties were contributing factors in determining student success (Boughan, 1998).

Administering surveys to current and former students is another popular means of assessing student preparation for transfer. Beyond the information that can be obtained from the institutions, student surveys can provide additional illumination into the transfer process and perceptions of effectiveness. One study of African American students entering a predominantly white university solicited information about the individuals considered to have an influence on the students' persistence and student participation in support and social organizations (Rodriguez and others, 1995). Satisfaction with academic experiences at the community college, especially in relation to how well it prepares the student for the transfer process and the requirements of the four-year institution, is frequently assessed (Conklin, 1995; Frank, 1998; Harbin, 1997; Mohammadi, Shaffer, and Farris, 1995). Student responses have also been solicited to assess the adjustment process after transfer (Laanan, 1997).

Most of the published studies rely on questionnaires specifically created for the particular analysis, but a number of researchers (Ackerman, 1990; Glover, 1996; Preston, 1993; Sworder, 1992) have used the Community College Student Experiences Questionnaire (CCSEQ) (Friedlander, Pace, and Lehman, 1990). The CCSEQ measures students' self-reported progress in six areas: (1) career preparation, (2) perspectives of the world, (3) personal and social development, (4) the arts, (5) communication skills, and (6) mathematics, science, and technology. It is intended for use in evaluating general education, transfer, and vocational programs, and it measures student interest, impressions, and satisfaction (*Community College Student Experiences Questionnaire*, 2000).

Qualitative studies are reported much less frequently in the literature, despite the assertion that they "can help us uncover the right questions, the questions raised by our students and ourselves about what we are doing and whether we are accomplishing our goals" (Mittler and Bers, 1994, p. 62). Those that appear are likely to rely on interviews, focus groups, or, occasionally, case studies of a particular college or program rather than participant observation as the chosen data collection method. A number of researchers spoke with students in order to identify what worked in the transfer process and what the community college could do to make the transfer process more effective (Davies and Casey, 1998; Townsend, 1995). Interviews conducted with faculty members, administrators, and students at the City College of San Francisco (*Traveling the Transfer Path*, 1998) helped identify the role of the faculty and the barriers to transfer. A few examples are available of researchers using both methodologies, usually conducting interviews or focus groups to clarify or expand on issues raised by survey responses (Allard, 1992; Kozeracki and Gerdeman, 2000; Nolan and Hall, 1974).

The Questions

The number of issues addressed in studies related to transfer students is extensive. A large number of studies about transfer students in the database focus on the following descriptive question: Who are the students and how do they perform academically? Some of the specific data collected to answer these questions—either for a single institution, a system, a state, or the country—include:

- Gender, race, age, socioeconomic status, major or program, and full- or part-time status (often cross-tabulated with other findings)
- Student goals and aspirations
- Impact of completing general education requirements or having to take developmental courses
- Effects of special programs, such as honors programs, and choice of major on achievement
- Grades (at the two- and the four-year institution)
- Number of credits attempted and received
- Withdrawal, persistence, graduation, and transfer rates
- Time to degree

(Arnold and Ugale, 1996; Boughan, 1995; Carlan and Byxbe, 2000; Glass and Bunn, 1998; Kearney, Townsend, and Kearney, 1995; Laanan, 1999; Lucas, Hull, and Brantley, 1995; Rice, 1996).

As previously mentioned, student satisfaction with the programs, policies, and services of the community college is commonly assessed (Conklin, 1995; Frank, 1998; Harbin, 1997; Mohammadi, Shaffer, and Farris, 1995). Other researchers compare the performance of transfer students with that of native students (Anglin, Davis, and Mooradian, 1995; Cejda and Kaylor, 1997; Dupraw and Michael, 1995; Hollomon and Snowden, 1996; Porter, 1999). These reports find support for the existence of transfer shock, evidenced by a dip in grades during the first semester or year after transfer, but those who examine the long-term achievements tend to conclude that transfer students ultimately perform almost as well as native students, in terms of GPA, at the time of graduation.

Some researchers have analyzed why students drop out and do not achieve their goals, including transfer (Cathey and Moody, 1994; *No Show Student Survey,* 1995; Sigworth, 1995; Timmons, 1978). Demographic data are usually collected and personal factors contributing to dropping out are presented, including financial need, work obligations, illness or other personal reasons, and dissatisfaction with instruction at the college.

Other researchers have investigated the transfer process from an institutional perspective: defining a consistent measure for transfer, describing different types of transfer, and identifying institutional factors that impede or foster transfer. A number of studies examine the definition of transfer itself—how the transfer rate is derived—in order to assess its validity (Cohen and Brawer, 1996; Rasor and Barr, 1995; Spicer and Armstrong, 1996). Cohen created a definition for a transfer rate in 1989, which has since been adopted by other researchers: "All students entering the community college in a given year who have no prior college experience and who complete at least 12 college credit units within four years, divided into the number of that group who take one or more classes at a public, in-state university or college within four years" (Cohen, 1996, p. 28). This number has remained between 21 and 24 percent for the last ten years (Center for the Study of Community Colleges, 2000). Other researchers have used different criteria to track the movement of students from community colleges to four-year institutions (Laanan and Sanchez, 1996). One drawback of this definition is that it is largely limited to the "vertical" transfer process (one community college to one four-year institution) of traditional students, a process that is not followed by all transfer students.

Researchers have become interested in the variety of transfer movements made by students. A number of studies (Adelman, 1999; Kinnick and others, 1997) found "the pattern of student movement between the community college and the university to be complex rather than straightforward" (Kinnick and others, 1997, p. 15). Thus, researchers have expanded the concept of transfer to include the phenomena of "reverse transfer" and "transfer swirl," which describe the movements of undergraduate students who begin their studies at a four-year institution and then transfer to a two-year institution, those who take community college classes while they are enrolled at a four-year institution, and four-year college graduates who enroll at a community college for personal development or career improvement (Townsend, 1999). These studies have explored the academic outcomes of these students and the impact of their presence on the community college classroom. Adelman (1999) points out that it is difficult to analyze institutional effects when students attend multiple institutions. "It is not wise to blame a college with superficially low graduation rates for the behavior of students who swirl through the system" (p. ix).

Factors that impede or support the success of transfer students have also been examined. Palmer (cited in Watkins, 1990) characterized the bureaucratic hurdles faced by transfer students as daunting. "One reason community-college students are less likely to get a B.A. is because they have to transfer. It's like going from Washington to Los Angeles and transferring in Chicago. You might miss the plane." A lack of appropriate guidance can compound these difficulties. Kinnick and others (1997) looked at the loss of credit between the community college and the university. They found that students' low grades, their attempts to transfer too many credits, or their enrollment in courses not intended for transfer (technical and developmental courses) are responsible for most of the credit loss rather than poor articulation between institutions. Articulation agreements—both those forged at the state level and those created by the faculty at individual institutions—have become more common as a tool for simplifying the transfer process (Cicarelli, 1993; Palmer, 1996; Robertson and Frier, 1996).

Model Studies

If the achievements of transfer students are being studied for the purpose of improving their outcomes and increasing the effectiveness of the community college in preparing them to transfer, several things should be considered in the design of the research. First, issues to be investigated should be ones over which the college has control so that it can address any identified problems. Murrell and Glover (1996) point out that "the investigation of the interaction between students and community college environments is often missing from outcomes assessment efforts. More attention is paid to comparing preusage variables such as age, ethnicity, entering test scores, grade point average and other exit criteria. Knowledge about what learners do and how they respond to an institution's efforts to provide a rich educational environment can add an important dimension in determining the impact of the educational experience" (p. 199). Second, the survey, interview, or focus group questions should be specific enough to allow action to be taken in response to evidence of problems. For example, a question asking whether the financial aid office provides sufficient guidance on applying for aid at the four-year institution is more helpful than asking whether students are satisfied with their experience with the financial aid office. It would be difficult to know what changes to make if the responses to the latter question were "not satisfied." Third, those individuals at the college whose department or work is being evaluated should be consulted during the process of designing the study so as to increase the likelihood of their being willing to respond to issues raised by the research. Following are examples of studies, questionnaires, and interview protocols that incorporate some or all of these elements and can serve as models for other community colleges to follow. In all cases, the complete survey instrument or interview protocols are included in the article.

Cohen and Brawer (1996) looked at pairs of colleges within the same state to determine why one has a high transfer rate (above 25 percent) and a neighboring college has a low transfer rate (below 15 percent). Their methodology includes both questionnaires distributed to the faculty members and students and interviews conducted with college administrators. Questions are specific enough to provide useful information: What particular student services tend to facilitate transfer on this campus? How are students informed about available financial aid? Aside from their actual teaching, what direct input do faculty members make to students who expect to transfer? Similarly, the recommendations at the end of the report are specific and practical, including the assertion that the colleges should emphasize transfer through such means as the college newspaper and the presidents' speeches, and that faculty members can play a key role in the transfer process by providing transfer-related information to students and participating in exchange programs with the university faculty.

The interview questions used with a small group of transfer students (Townsend, 1995) appear to be very effective in identifying specific sources of difficulty in the transfer adjustment process. The questions, which address the responsibility of the student for his or her own progress as well as the community college and the university role, include the following:

- Did you receive any assistance at the community college when you decided to transfer to the university? Did you ask for any?
- Is there anything the university should do to better aid students who want to transfer?
- Is the university different from the community college as far as academics are concerned? If so, how is it different?
- Are the testing procedures used by teachers at the university different from the procedures used by the community college?
- Do you feel that the community college prepared you to do well academically at the university? If not, what might it have done differently?

These specific questions allowed the researcher to derive some interesting and practical findings. For example, she concluded that community colleges, with their student-centered approach designed to build self-esteem, "may contribute to the confusion and shock of transfer [of] students facing different standards and expectations at the university" (Townsend, 1995, p. 189). Therefore, community college faculty members might want to consider increasing writing assignments and essay tests, and they might want to talk with students about the probability of their entering a more rigorous environment after transfer.

A group of faculty members at Big Bend Community College (BBCC) took on the role of researchers by interviewing former students who had transferred to Washington State University, in order to assess how effectively the community college had prepared students for transfer and continued success at the university (Allard, 1992). Before the interviews, the students completed a short questionnaire, ranking their experience and evaluation of BBCC. During the interviews, the students were asked to recommend changes in specific areas of the community college to improve transfer preparation. Although the questions were broad—such as "What could we have done more of, or better, that would have helped you do well at WSU?" and "What can we change at BBCC to better serve students?"—the interview format elicited specific, doable recommendations, including: require more papers/research papers, provide more information on transferring and clarify four-year school requirements for specific majors, provide more exposure to computers and word processing, and require more essay exams and term papers.

A fourth useful study was based on the premise that traditional research on transfer students, which uses the student as the unit of analysis, does not create the incentive to act among faculty members, as they cannot change the students' background or make them complete at least thirty hours before transferring (Quanty, Dixon, and Ridley, 1996). This study proposes a course-based model of transfer success that shows how well students who complete course prerequisites at a community college perform in specific courses, compared with students who complete the prerequisites at the receiving college. The researchers developed a tracking system that examines every course having a prerequisite that can be met at the community college or the four-year institution. Grade distributions are produced and are broken out by whether the prerequisite was taken at the university or the community college. The researchers found that students who completed the prerequisites at the community college performed at a level equal to or higher than that of the students who completed the course at the university. Beyond that, "the real strength of [the] new paradigm is that when a problem is identified it can be pinpointed to a specific course at the community college and at the receiving college. Faculty take ownership [of] students who have successfully completed their course(s). If those students are not prepared for subsequent coursework, faculty want to know why" (p. 4). Generally, this information is available from all higher education institutions, making this study easy to replicate.

Another study also focused on the involvement of faculty members, looking at their role in facilitating the academic success of transfer students (Cejda, 1998). It describes a collaborative effort developed between faculty members at a liberal arts college and faculty members at five community colleges to "develop a seamless four-year educational program, assuming that a student would complete the AA degree at the community college and transfer to the liberal arts college to complete the baccalaureate degree" (p. 72). Professors in nine of the liberal arts college's eighteen departments collaborated with their community college counterparts to develop curriculum guides specifying the courses that had to be taken for a particular major at the community college and the four-year liberal arts college. Data about the grades and bachelor's degree attainment of students who transferred from a community college that had developed a curriculum guide were collected and compared with those of a control group of transfer students in the same majors. Study findings indicated that the competency-based curriculum agreements facilitated the first-semester academic performance of community college transfer students, as measured by GPA, and contributed to a higher proportion of students attaining a bachelor's degree.

Finally, following is a presentation of examples of interesting and useful questions that have been used in a variety of questionnaires administered to students, the responses to which are likely to initiate action to improve transfer preparation. One survey of "no show" students concluded with the question "Would you like someone from the Schoolcraft College to contact you regarding courses?" and requested the individual's name and address (*No Show Student Survey,* 1995). At many community colleges, some students with the expressed intent to transfer dropped out for a variety of work- and family-related reasons. Following up with these students and showing them that the college is interested in their academic progress may be an effective way to bring them back to campus.

A survey distributed to graduates of Westchester Community College (Hankin and Ford, 1995) includes examples of questions that are too broadly worded to be of real assistance: "To what extent do you feel WCC prepared you for further study?"—and specific questions that could guide reform: "How effective was your experience at WCC in developing skills in expressing [your]self in writing?" and "To what extent are you satisfied with your experience [with] academic advising by academic faculty?"

St. Augustine College, which has a high proportion of Hispanic students, includes on its Graduating Student Exit Survey the following question: "How do you feel about your command of English in the following areas? (1–5 satisfaction scale) Reading the newspaper. Reading college texts. Writing a letter. Writing a paper for class. Listening to a conversation. Listening to a lecture. Speaking in a conversation. Speaking to a group. Speaking in a class." Although this question might not be relevant to all community colleges, it is most certainly appropriate and actionable at a college that boasts of being a "Pioneer in Bilingualism."

Camden County College's one-year graduate follow-up survey asks students to specify the problems they encountered in transferring to their four-year institution—such as transferring credit hours, transcript problems, and admissions problems. If a large number of students had problems with transferring credit hours or sending transcripts, these issues could be traced to and addressed by the appropriate department (Camden County College, 1995).

Making Use of the Data

A substantial amount of quantitative and qualitative data about transfer students has been collected by researchers at the community colleges and the four-year institutions. Much of this information is descriptive in nature. Both the characteristics of the students and the nature of the transfer process have been explored. In some cases, research findings are supplemented by recommendations that provide guidance for implementing changes in response to the results of the study. Unfortunately, in many cases, data are reported to fulfill state requirements or researchers' agendas and may never be used by those responsible for administering college departments and programs. Building a link between research and action is the responsibility of both the people who collect the data and the practitioners who oversee the programs at the colleges. It is hoped that the model studies presented here will serve as examples of how to use research to improve the academic outcomes of transfer students.

References

Ackerman, S. P. *A Comparison of a Sub-Population of Santa Monica College Students to Other Community College Students in the Southern California Area: An Analysis of the Results from the Community College Student Experiences Questionnaire.* Santa Monica, Calif.: Santa Monica College, 1990. (ED 315 132)

Adams, J. "Learning from Transfer Data Exchange." *Michigan Community College Journal: Research and Practice,* 1999, 5(2), 53–67.

Adelman, C. *Answers in the Tool Box: Academic Intensity, Attendance Patterns, and Bachelor's Degree Attainment.* Washington, D.C.: Office of Educational Research and Improvement, U.S. Department of Education, 1999,

Alexander, H. *Graduate Follow-Up Survey, FY94.* Research Brief RB96–14. Largo, Md.: Prince George's Community College, 1996. (ED 395 648)

Allard, S. *Transfer Student Follow-Up: Washington State University Students Reflect upon Big Bend Community College Education.* Moses Lake, Wash.: Big Bend Community College, 1992. (ED 344 637)

Anglin, L. W., Davis, J. W., and Mooradian, P. W. "Do Transfer Students Graduate? A Comparative Study of Transfer Students and Native University Students." *Community College Journal of Research and Practice,* 1995, 19, 321–330.

Arnold, C. L., and Ugale, R. *Student Outcomes Report: The Latest Numbers and Recent Trends in Student Success, Withdrawal, Persistence, Degrees/Certificates, and Transfer, Fall 1996.* Hayward, Calif.: Chabot College, 1996. (ED 421 196)

Articulation Accountability Committee of the Articulation Coordinating Committee. *Florida Articulation Summary.* Tallahassee, Fla.: Articulation Accountability Committee of the Articulation Coordinating Committee, 1998. (ED 418 762)

Blau, J. R. "Two-Year College Transfer Rates of Black American Students." *Community College Journal of Research and Practice,* 1999, 23, 525–531.

Boughan, K. *Tracking Student Progress at PGCC: Basic Findings of the 1990 Entering Cohort, Four-Year Academic Outcome Analysis.* Enrollment Analysis EA95–7. Largo, Md.: Prince George's Community College, 1995. (ED 382 273)

Boughan, K. "New Approaches to the Analysis of Academic Outcomes: Modeling Student Performance at a Community College." Paper presented at the annual forum of the Association for Institutional Research, Minneapolis, Minn., 1998. (ED 424 798)

Camden County College. *Camden County College One-Year Graduate Follow-Up Survey: 1993 Graduates.* Camden, N.J.: Camden County College, 1995. (ED 387 178)

Carlan, P. E., and Byxbe, F. R. "Community Colleges Under the Microscope: An Analysis of Performance Predictors for Native and Transfer Students." *Community College Review,* 2000, 28(2), 27–42.

Cathey, S. A., and Moody, B. *Garland County Community College Non-Returning Survey.* Hot Springs, Ariz.: Garland County Community College, 1994. (ED 369 462)

Cejda, B. D. "An Examination of Transfer Shock in Academic Disciplines." *Community College Journal of Research and Practice,* 1997, *21,* 279–288.

Cejda, B. D. "Faculty Collaboration and Competency-Based Curriculum Agreements: Meaningful Links in Transfer Education." *Michigan Community College Journal: Research and Practice,* 1998, 4(1), 69–78.

Cejda, B. D., and Kaylor, A. J. "Academic Performance of Community College Transfer Students at Private Liberal Arts Colleges." *Community College Journal of Research and Practice,* 1997, *21,* 651–659.

Center for the Study of Community Colleges. *Results of the 1999 Transfer Assembly.* Los Angeles: Center for the Study of Community Colleges, 2000.

Cicarelli, J. "The Problems of Transfer Students." *Chronicle of Higher Education,* 1993. [http://www.chronicle.com].

Cohen, A. M. "Orderly Thinking About a Chaotic System." In T. Rifkin (ed.), *Transfer and Articulation: Improving Policies to Meet New Needs.* New Directions for Community Colleges, no. 96. San Francisco: Jossey-Bass, 1996.

Cohen, A. M., and Brawer, F. B. *Policies and Programs That Affect Transfer.* Washington, D.C.: American Council on Education, 1996. (ED 385 336)

Community College Student Experiences Questionnaire. [http://www.people.memphis.edu/%7Ecoe_cshe/CCSEQ_main.htm]. 2000.

Community College Transfer Performance at JMU. Harrisonburg, Va.: James Madison University, 1998. (ED 434 714)

Conklin, K. A. *Community College Students' Persistence and Goal Attainment: A Five-Year Longitudinal Study.* AIR Professional File, No. 55. 1995. (ED 384 404)

Davies, T. G., and Casey, K. L. "Student Perceptions of the Transfer Process: Strengths, Weaknesses, and Recommendations for Improvement." *Journal of Applied Research in the Community College,* 1998, *5,* 101–110.

Duckwall, J. M. *JCCC Transfer Students: Their Destinations and Achievements.* Overland Park, Kans.: Johnson County Community College, 1997. (ED 405 061)

Dupraw, C., and Michael, W. B. "Community College Transfer Students: Comparing Admission and Success." *College and University,* 1995, 71(2), 10–18.

Frank, J. *Howard Community College's 1992–1996 Transfer Graduates: A Trend Analysis.* Columbia, Md.: Howard Community College, 1998. (ED 431 453)

Friedlander, J., Pace, C. R., and Lehman, P. W. *The Community College Student Experience Questionnaire.* Los Angeles: Center for the Study of Student Evaluation, University of California, 1990.

Glass, J. C., Jr., and Bunn, C. E. "Length of Time Required to Graduate for Community College Students Transferring to Senior Institutions." *Community College Journal of Research and Practice,* 1998, *22,* 239–261.

Glover, J. W. "Campus Environment and Student Involvement as Predictors of Outcomes of the Community College Experience." Paper presented at the annual meeting of the Association for the Study of Higher Education, Memphis, Tenn., Nov. 1996. (ED 402 831)

The Graduate Survey, 1992–1993. St. Petersburg, Fla.: St. Petersburg Junior College, 1995. (ED 391 544)

Grosset, J. *An Assessment of Community College of Philadelphia's Effectiveness in Preparing Students for Transfer and Employment.* Institutional Research Report no. 92. Philadelphia: Community College of Philadelphia, 1996. (ED 412 991)

Hankin, J. N., and Ford, J. C. *Westchester Community College Graduate Study.* Valhalla, N.Y.: Westchester Community College, 1995. (ED 391 564)

Harbin, C. E. "A Survey of Transfer Students at Four-Year Institutions Serving a California Community College." *Community College Review,* 1997, 25(2), 21–40.

Hollomon, C. A., and Snowden, M. *Comparing Performance of Two-Year Community College Students to Four-Year Native Students.* Hattiesburg: University of Southern Mississippi, 1996. (ED 403 005)

Hoyt, J. E. "Promoting Student Transfer Success: Curriculum Evaluation and Student Academic Preparation." *Journal of Applied Research in the Community College,* 1999, 6(2), 73–79.

Illinois Community College Board. *Student Enrollments and Completions in the Illinois Community College System, Fiscal Year 1997.* Springfield: Illinois Community College Board, 1998. (ED 415 926)

Kearney, G. W., Townsend, B. K., and Kearney, T. J. "Multiple-Transfer Students in a Public Urban University: Background Characteristics and Interinstitutional Movements." *Research in Higher Education,* 1995, 36, 323–344.

Kent Trumbull Student Transfer Behavior: Survey Results, Conclusions, and Implications. Warren, Ohio: Kent State University, 1995. (ED 388 329)

Kinnick, M. K., and others. "Student Transfer and Outcomes Between Community Colleges and a University in an Urban Environment." Paper presented at the annual forum of the Association for Institutional Research, Orlando, Fla., May 1997. (ED 410 895)

Kozeracki, C. A., and Gerdeman, R. D. "Transfer Readiness Research Project Focus Group Findings." Unpublished report. University of California, Los Angeles, 2000.

Laanan, F. S. "Making the Transition: Understanding the Adjustment Process of Community College Transfer Students." *Community College Review,* 1996, 23(4), 69–84.

Laanan, F. S. *From Community College to University: A Comparative Study of Santa Monica College and Non–Santa Monica College Students.* Santa Monica, Calif.: Santa Monica College, 1997. (ED 437 098)

Laanan, F. S. "Does Age Matter? A Study of Transfer Students' College Experience and Adjustment Process." Paper presented at the annual forum of the Association for Institutional Research, Seattle, June 1999. (ED 433 788)

Laanan, F. S., and Sanchez, J. R. "New Ways of Conceptualizing Transfer Rate Definitions." In T. Rifkin (ed.), *Transfer and Articulation: Improving Policies to Meet New Needs.* New Directions for Community Colleges, no. 96. San Francisco: Jossey-Bass, 1996.

Lanni, J. C. "Modeling Student Outcomes: A Longitudinal Study." Paper presented at the annual forum of the Association for Institutional Research, Orlando, Fla., May 1997.

Lucas, J. A., Hull, E., and Brantley, F. *Follow-Up Study of Students Taking Honors Courses, 1990–1995.* Palatine, Ill.: William Rainey Harper College, 1995. (ED 397 904)

McCormick, A. C., and Carroll, C. D. *Transfer Behavior Among Beginning Postsecondary Students, 1989–94.* Washington, D.C.: U.S. Department of Education, 1997. (ED 408 929)

Minear, D. J. "Models for Understanding and Predicting the Undergraduate Educational Attainment Patterns of Public Community College Students Who Transfer with the Associate in Arts Degree into a State University System." Unpublished doctoral dissertation. Florida State University, Tallahassee, 1998. (ED 427 809)

Mittler, M. L., and Bers, T. H. "Qualitative Assessment: An Institutional Reality Check." In T. H. Bers and M. L. Mittler (eds.), *Assessment and Testing: Myths and Realities.* New Directions for Community Colleges, no. 88. San Francisco: Jossey-Bass, 1994. (ED 376 900)

Mohammadi, J., Shaffer, B., and Farris, R. *Academic Performance of PHCC Students Transferring to Institutions of Higher Education.* Martinsville, Va.: Patrick Henry Community College, 1995. (ED 382 260)

Murrell, P. H., and Glover, J. W. "The Community College Experience: Assessing Process and Progress." *Community College Journal of Research and Practice,* 1996, 20, 199–200.

No Show Student Survey. Livonia, Miss.: Schoolcraft College, 1995. (ED 387 188)

Nolan, E. J., and Hall, D. L. *A Follow-Up Study of Transfer Students from Southern West Virginia Community College to Marshall University.* Logan: Southern West Virginia Community College, 1974. (ED 114 139)

North Carolina Community College System. *Critical Success Factors for the North Carolina Community College System, 1995. Sixth Annual Report.* Raleigh: North Carolina Community College System, 1995. (ED 387 185)

Palmer, J. C. "Transfer as a Function of Interinstitutional Faculty Deliberations." In T. Rifkin (ed.), *Transfer and Articulation: Improving Policies to Meet New Needs*. New Directions for Community Colleges, no. 96. San Francisco: Jossey-Bass, 1996.

Porter, S. "Assessing Transfer and Native Student Performance at Four-Year Institutions." Paper presented at the annual forum of the Association for Institutional Research, Seattle, June 1999. (ED 433 790)

Preston, D. L. "Using the CCSEQ in Institutional Effectiveness: The Role of Goal Commitment and Student's Perception of Gains." Paper presented at the annual forum of the Association for Institutional Research, Chicago, May 1993. (ED 360 022)

Quanty, M. B., Dixon, R. W., and Ridley, D. R. "The Course-Based Model of Transfer Success: An Action-Oriented Research Paradigm." Paper presented at the annual conference of the Southeastern Association for Community College Research, Panama City, Fla., Aug. 1996. (ED 397 864)

Rasor, R. A., and Barr, J. E. *The Transfer Eligible Rate: Longitudinal Results of a Companion Measure to the Transfer Rate*. Sacramento, Calif.: American River College, 1995. (ED 390 484)

Rice, S. "Evaluating the 'Colorado Core Transfer Program' as Public Policy." *Michigan Community College Journal: Research and Practice,* 1996, 2(2), 63–72.

Robertson, P. F., and Frier, T. "The Role of the State in Transfer and Articulation." In T. Rifkin (ed.), *Transfer and Articulation: Improving Policies to Meet New Needs*. New Directions for Community Colleges, no. 96. San Francisco: Jossey-Bass, 1996.

Rodriguez, J. C., and others. "Intragroup Differences Between Black Native and Transfer Students at a Predominantly White University: Implications for Advising." *NACADA Journal,* 1995, 15(1), 31–35.

Saupe, J. L., and Long, S. "Admissions Standards for Undergraduate Transfer Students: A Policy Analysis." Paper presented at the annual forum of the Association for Institutional Research, Albuquerque, N.Mex., May 1996. (ED 397 720)

Sigworth, D. *Student Withdrawal Study, Schoolcraft College*. Livonia, Miss.: Schoolcraft College, 1995. (ED 387 186)

Spicer, S. L., and Armstrong, W. B. "Transfer: The Elusive Denominator." In T. Rifkin (ed.), *Transfer and Articulation: Improving Policies to Meet New Needs*. New Directions for Community Colleges, no. 96. San Francisco: Jossey-Bass, 1996. (ED 400 912)

State Board of Directors for Community Colleges of Arizona. *Report to Arizona, 1999.* Phoenix: State Board of Directors for Community Colleges of Arizona, 1999. (ED 437 105)

Sworder, S. *Analysis of the Survey of Student Experiences at Saddleback College via the Community College Student Experiences Questionnaire (CCSEQ). Saddleback College Accreditation '92*. Mission Viejo, Calif.: Saddleback College, 1992. (ED 339 445)

Timmons, F. R. "Freshman Withdrawal from College: A Positive Step Toward Identity Formation? A Follow-Up Study." *Journal of Youth and Adolescence,* 1978, 7, 159–173.

Townsend, B. K. "Community College Transfer Students: A Case Study of Survival." *Review of Higher Education,* 1995, 18, 175–193.

Townsend, B. K. (ed.). *Understanding the Impact of Reverse Transfer Students on Community Colleges*. New Directions for Community Colleges, no. 106. San Francisco: Jossey-Bass, 1999.

Traveling the Transfer Path: Student Experiences at City College of San Francisco. San Francisco: City College of San Francisco, 1998. (ED 416 946)

U.S. Department of Education. *Subbaccalaureate Persistence and Attainment: Indicator of the Month*. NCES 98–001. Washington, D.C.: U.S. Department of Education, 1997. (ED 411 918)

Walters, J. E., and Shymoniak, L. *The Effectiveness of California Community Colleges on Selected Performance Measures, October 1996*. Sacramento: Chancellor's Office, California Community Colleges, 1996. (ED 401 959)

Watkins, B. T. "Two-Year Institutions Under Pressure to Ease Transfers." *Chronicle of Higher Education,* Feb. 7, 1990. [http://www.chronicle.com].

CAROL A. KOZERACKI is assistant director for publications and special projects at the ERIC Clearinghouse for Community Colleges and a doctoral candidate in higher education at the University of California, Los Angeles.

7

This chapter addresses the motivating factors that led to research and collaboration efforts to uncover issues pertaining to transfer students at one community college in Southern California. Implications and ongoing research are discussed.

Transfer Readiness: A Case Study of Former Santa Monica College Students

Brenda Johnson-Benson, Peter B. Geltner,
Steven K. Steinberg

For many community colleges, transfer is an important part of the institutional mission. For some, it seems to be the most important goal. Certainly, that has been true for many years at Santa Monica College (SMC), which prides itself on the number of students it sends to local public and private universities. Students often come to SMC, they say, because of the reputation SMC has for helping students transfer; furthermore, they come from all over the country and the world. From 1994–95 through 1998–99, the numbers of SMC students enrolled in the following California public and private four-year institutions were as follows: University of California (UC), 3,191; California State University (CSU), 4,217; and University of Southern California (USC), 594.

The project profiled in this chapter began back in 1995 as a conversation between colleagues. It is important to understand the genesis of the project so that others may find a way to do what we have done and perhaps avoid some of the problems we faced. Also, we hope that others will replicate—and improve upon—our model. For example, we have come to understand how unusual it is to have someone from the teaching faculty be involved in the study of transfer. We also more fully understand how important that synergy is, and how important it is to maintain a dialogue across the boundaries traditionally found between academics and student services personnel.

First, we will provide some background about how the project began. Then we will discuss the stages we went through to develop our methodology, including the populations we studied and the process by which we have continued to fine-tune the project. We will conclude by discussing some of

New Directions for Community Colleges, no. 114, Summer 2001 © John Wiley & Sons, Inc.

the results obtained thus far, plans for the next phases of the project, and implications for practice from three different perspectives.

Background

This five-year project arose from several different constituencies within Santa Monica College. In 1995, the new incoming president of SMC, Piedad Robertson, had expressed an interest in finding out how well SMC students did, once they transferred. She commissioned the assistant dean of transfer, Brenda Johnson-Benson, to undertake a study of former SMC students' experiences at local colleges and universities. At approximately the same time, an English teacher, Steven Steinberg, had been doing research on the question of transfer in preparation for his doctoral dissertation on community college missions. He wondered how many SMC students were actually going on to receive bachelor's or other degrees. In the course of his research, he realized that he was not sure if he, himself, was adequately preparing his students for the kind of work they would encounter, once they transferred. He went to the assistant dean of transfer with his questions. They both realized that the kinds of data and statistics many take for granted did not seem to be readily available, and that some kind of study would be good for the college, and certainly would benefit the students. They set up a meeting to discuss it further, inviting the dean of institutional research, Peter Geltner, who readily agreed to attend.

At that first meeting, we realized that we wanted to know more than just the number of SMC students who transferred and received their baccalaureate degree. We felt that we needed to assess ourselves further, beyond the basic transfer statistics, to ask transfer students how SMC had really helped them, and what might we have done better in terms of academic preparation, counseling, and related areas. As a logical place to start, we decided to call a number of people at UCLA, at various levels, to ask how many SMC students had actually gone on to receive baccalaureate degrees over the past five years. Much to our surprise, nobody knew. We tried other avenues throughout the entire UC system, to no avail. It was then that we understood that we had stumbled upon a deeper question than we had realized, and we decided to begin the project.

The Project

The first two years of the project were funded by Santa Monica College. The purpose of the first session was to get a preliminary sense of the concerns of the students and to try out a number of questions. Former SMC students who were enrolled at UCLA were invited to talk with a group of interested faculty members and administrators who wanted to know more about their experiences at both SMC and UCLA. SMC department chairs, counselors, and teachers were on hand to interview students from a number of different majors, with a prearranged set of open-ended questions. Most students were rather enthusiastic about their experience at SMC, but they also had a number of concrete suggestions and comments regarding academic preparation, counseling, and institutional priorities.

We incorporated their ideas into our first survey questionnaire. The survey instrument used to collect data for the UCLA pilot study was developed by Laanan (1998). Called the UCLA Transfer Students' Questionnaire (UCLA-TSQ), the 304-item instrument was formulated as a result of extensive review of past survey instruments and previous studies in the area (Astin, 1993; Baker and Siryk, 1984, 1986; Laanan, 1995; Pace, 1990, 1992). Specifically, the instrument measured transfer students' noncognitive or affective traits—attitudes, values, and interests—in different areas.

In the first section pertaining to SMC, there were questions regarding the rigorousness of coursework, satisfaction with the transfer/counseling center, experiences with faculty members and written assignments, and learning and study skills. The section on UCLA focused on general perceptions, the adjustment process, college satisfaction, and estimate of gains. Above all, we wanted data that would be useful to teachers, counselors, and administrators, for the overall good of the students and the college. We all understood that we needed a mechanism to query and listen to the students, and then to communicate those results back to our colleagues. As community college practitioners, we knew how important praxis would be to this project, if changes were to be made.

Before we get to the development of the project, we should note that the preliminary results we obtained from the first round of questionnaires with the UCLA students (year two) were quite helpful in formulating and expanding the project. In some ways, the results were even more positive than the subsequent results, and there were also some surprising and important revelations. For example, we found that one of every thirteen upper-division students at UCLA, as of 1998, was an SMC transfer student, and we began to think about the implications of those kinds of statistics.

After the second year, we expanded the project to include five additional four-year schools. The goal was to include both smaller and larger, as well as public and private, institutions. For year three, data were collected using a survey instrument similar to the one used in the UCLA pilot study. The major difference was that the survey, called the SMC Transfer Students' Questionnaire (SMC-TSQ), included only 103 items. Originally developed by Laanan (1998) and modified for this follow-up, the SMC-TSQ (Laanan, 1999) is a comprehensive instrument that measures transfer students' experiences (academic and social, cognitive and affective outcomes) in the two- and four-year environments. For the third-year follow-up study of former SMC students at five public and private four-year institutions (California State University, Northridge; Loyola Marymount University; Mount Saint Mary's College; Pepperdine University; and the University of Southern California), modifications were made to the TSQ as a result of the UCLA pilot study conducted during year two of the project. It is important to note that the TSQ for the third-year project was slightly different from the instrument used in the UCLA study.

Brenda secured three-year funding from the California Community Colleges Chancellor's Office (CCCCO) so that we would be able to look at additional cohorts over a longer period of time. The project sequence was as follows:

Year One: Open-ended interviews at UCLA

Year Two: Written surveys mailed to 945 UCLA students

Year Three (first year of grant funding from CCCCO): Written surveys mailed to transfer students at California State University, Northridge (CSUN), Loyola Marymount University (LMU), Mount St. Mary's College (MSMC), Pepperdine University (PU), and the University of Southern California (USC)

Year Four: Focus groups conducted at all five institutions; SMC Transfer Advisory Committee established

Year Five (2000–01, final year of funding): Departmental dialogues between faculty members at SMC and UCLA

For the UCLA study conducted in year two of the project, 945 surveys were mailed to students who transferred to UCLA. A total of 292 students responded, yielding a response rate of 31 percent. In year three, surveys were mailed to 1,536 students at the five institutions. A total of 442 usable completed surveys were received, a response rate of 29 percent. For this chapter, only identical data elements that appeared in both the UCLA pilot study and the SMC-TSQ are presented. The results presented here are therefore based on a sample of 734 former SMC students—292 from the UCLA pilot study and 442 from the third follow-up study—who transferred to different four-year institutions.

The first results were quite intriguing (see Table 7.1). For example, overall, the students seemed satisfied with their training in critical/analytical thinking, preparation for four-year academic standards and four-year majors, and information regarding admissions requirements.

However, the students seemed less satisfied with their overall reading preparation than they were with their writing preparation. They also seemed less satisfied with counseling assistance in the application process. Though we expected a relatively low response, we were nonetheless quite surprised at how few had received transfer/career guidance from the teaching faculty. This confirmed for us that the teaching faculty do not see themselves in this role.

Research in one area—financial aid information—has already led to positive changes. For some time, different departments at SMC had been investigating better ways to deliver this information to students. The results served as a catalyst, opening lines of communications between departments, which, in turn, resulted in departmental cross-training and new, more efficient delivery methods.

Table 7.1. Santa Monica College Experiences:
Responses to Selected Items (N = 734)

SMC Coursework[a]

Courses developed my critical and analytical thinking	74.8%
Courses required extensive reading assignments	58.5%
Courses prepared me for the academic standards at the four-year institution	75.1%
Courses prepared me for my major at the four-year institution	66.5%
Writing assignments/instruction prepared me for my work at the four-year institution	66.1%

Experiences with Faculty[a]

Encouraged me to discuss my transfer/career plans and ambitions	20.5%
Made me excited and interested in their academic discipline/area	48.1%

Learning and Study Skills[a]

"To what extent do you agree or disagree that your academic experience at SMC gave you the following skills you needed to prepare for the standards and academic rigor at the four-year institution":

Computer skills	35.6%
Writing skills	66.8%
Research skills	53.4%

SMC Transfer/Counselor Center[b]

Provided information regarding admission requirements to four-year institutions	62.8%
Provided assistance in the application process	38.9%
Provided information regarding financial aid	25.6%

Experience in Writing[c]

Very often wrote research papers in English and non-English courses	22.1%

[a]Percentage responding "somewhat agree" or "strongly agree." Responses were based on a 5-point scale: 1 = strongly disagree; 2 = somewhat disagree; 3 = neutral; 4 = somewhat agree; 5 = strongly agree.

[b]Percentage responding "somewhat helpful" or "very helpful." Responses were based on a 6-point scale: 1 = very unhelpful; 2 = somewhat unhelpful; 3 = neutral; 4 = somewhat helpful; 5 = very helpful; 6 = don't know, did not use service.

[c]Responses were based on a 4-point scale: 1 = never; 2 = occasionally; 3 = often; 4 = very often.

We were surprised to see that students felt a lack of preparation for research paper writing across the curriculum, and those perceptions partially carried over into other areas of writing.

Another area that led to additional questions revolved around the question of SMC teachers and their academic fields. At first glance, it looked as though the teachers were not "generating interest" in their own fields or encouraging students to major in those fields. However, focus groups revealed something quite different. Students acknowledged that teachers tended not to talk about those kinds of issues in the classroom, but they indicated that in smaller sessions or office conferences, teachers were much more likely to address those issues—and with enthusiasm.

The lack of computer skill preparation may be a bit misleading, as SMC embarked on an extensive campuswide purchase and upgrade program after the interviewees had transferred. Nevertheless, the results were startling, considering the importance of computers on the campus and in many careers.

The students, overall, really seemed to like SMC and seemed to feel that their preparation had enabled them to be confident of success at their four-year schools (see Tables 7.2 and 7.3). In fact, their apparent lack of transfer shock (or dip in grades) pleasantly surprised all of us.

Ongoing Research

As noted earlier, 2000–01 is the last year of the original funding. One of the requirements of that funding, and one of our most important goals from the very beginning, was to develop concrete recommendations for practice. The Transfer Education Advisory Committee, established during year four, developed and has begun to implement eight practical institutional recommendations as a result of the survey results and the extensive student focus group interviews. They are grouped under three main headings and can be summarized as follows:

1. Address reading and writing across the curriculum:

- Offer a series of workshops during the Fall 2000 flex day. (These were offered and were received with great enthusiasm by the faculty.)
- Encourage English department faculty members and those from other disciplines to schedule one to two hours per week in a writing lab or tutoring center.

2. Address computer literacy and information competency:

- Promote computer literacy by offering workshops on Internet usage and software packages to faculty members and students, across the curriculum. (Many new programs and workshops have been offered from a variety of sources on campus, and more are anticipated.)

3. Address student services and counseling issues:

- Provide extensive financial aid training for the academic counseling staff. (Instituted in Fall 2000.)
- Encourage the counseling department to create a comprehensive mission statement. (Completed in Spring 2000.)
- Create a policies and procedures manual, and provide better training for the entire counseling faculty. (Manual completed in Spring 2001; new training model developed in Fall 2000.)

**Table 7.2. Opinions About Santa Monica College:
Responses to Selected Items (N = 734)**

I *really liked* SMC.[a]	60.6%
If I could start my community college experience over again, *yes, definitely* I would choose SMC or the four-year institution for the first year or two.[b]	55.1%
Because of my academic preparation at SMC, I was confident that I would be successful at the four-year institution.[c]	70.0%

[a]Responses were based on a 5-point scale: 1 = I really didn't like it; 2 = I didn't like it; 3 = I am neutral about it; 4 = I liked it somewhat; 5 = I really liked SMC.

[b]Responses were based on a 5-point scale: 1 = definitely no; 2 = probably no; 3 = neutral; 4 = probably yes; 5 = definitely yes.

[c]Percentage responding "somewhat agree" or "strongly agree." Responses were based on a 5-point scale: 1 = strongly disagree; 2 = somewhat disagree; 3 = neutral; 4 = somewhat agree; 5 = strongly agree.

Table 7.3. University Experiences: Adjustment Process (N = 734)

Adjusting to the academic standards or expectations has been easy	57.3%
Adjusting to the social environment has been easy	59.5%
Over time, I became accustomed to the size of the student body	75.1%
I experienced a dip in grades (GPA) during the first or second semester	39.0%

Note: Percentage responding "somewhat agree" or "strongly agree." Responses were based on a 5-point scale: 1 = strongly disagree; 2 = somewhat disagree; 3 = neutral; 4 = somewhat agree; 5 = strongly agree.

- Develop brochures and other materials that clearly define and outline SMC counseling services, and distribute them widely to students and faculty and staff members. (Printed in early Fall 2000.) Redesign transfer/counseling Web site, as well. (Begun in Spring 2001.)
- Investigate alternative forums for providing counseling services. (Ongoing.)

This final year will see expanded communication between the faculty of SMC, UCLA, and other four-year institutions, with special cooperation from the UCLA Center for the Study of Community Colleges. We will also endeavor to disseminate our findings to colleagues at our own institution and will encourage increased participation across campus.

Implications for Practice

This study has had a major impact on the institutional research, counseling, and teaching functions of Santa Monica College. From the perspective of Institutional Research, this study has been really exciting. Most times, we tend to concentrate on transfer numbers provided by the state or the universities. At best, the universities might provide us with success numbers specific to our former students. On some occasions, we might even get grade information. However, rarely do we have the opportunity to connect the techniques and processes we use on campus to the success of students after they transfer. This project has given us a tremendous opportunity to do a more complete self-analysis.

The primary concern of community college transfer center directors nationwide is the number of students who transfer out of their institutions. For most campuses, both prestige and funding are tied to this number. Although it is important that a community college have a well-organized, proactive transfer center that facilitates and encourages community college students to transfer to four-year institutions, more emphasis needs to be placed on the qualitative side of the equation. What happens to students once they transfer? Were they well prepared academically? Did they receive the necessary support and guidance throughout the transfer process?

This research project attempted to answer these questions by querying the transfer students themselves. The answers we received helped us to adjust our curriculum, modify transfer student support services, and get instructional faculty members to talk about the content of their courses and the needs of their students. We strongly believe that every community college and four-year institution has a moral obligation to engage in a similar process to ensure the academic preparedness of its students.

The results from our research can inform the teaching practices within the college—from writing assignments to research papers to teaching style. The research highlights the important role that community college faculty members play in students' ability to succeed after transferring. With our increasingly diverse student population, and the increasingly important role of community colleges in higher education today, we need to make sure that our students are academically "transfer ready" in addition to possessing the right number of credits. Successful transfer, therefore, is very much a part of our academic responsibility, and we must see it in that context.

References

Astin, A. W. *What Matters in College? Four Critical Years Revisited.* San Francisco: Jossey-Bass, 1993.

Baker, R. W., and Siryk, B. "Measuring Adjustment to College." *Journal of Counseling Psychology,* 1984, *31,* 179–189.

Baker, R. W., and Siryk, B. "Exploratory Intervention with a Scale Measuring Adjustment to College." *Journal of Counseling Psychology,* 1986, *33,* 31–38.

Laanan, F. S. "Making the Transition: An Exploratory Study of Academic Achievement, Involvement, Adjustment, and Satisfaction of Transfer Students at UCLA." Report presented to the dean of the College of Letters and Science, University of California, Los Angeles, 1995. (ED 400 889)

Laanan, F. S. "Beyond Transfer Shock: A Study of Students' College Experiences and Adjustment Processes at UCLA." Unpublished doctoral dissertation, Graduate School of Education and Information Studies, University of California, Los Angeles, 1998.

Laanan, F. S. "Final Report: Transfer Readiness Research and Follow-Up Practices." Transfer Readiness Institutionalization Project, RFA no. 97-0601. Report to the California Community Colleges Chancellor's Office, Student Services and Special Programs Division. Santa Monica, Calif., Dec.17, 1999.

Pace, C. R. *College Student Experiences Questionnaire.* (3rd ed.) Los Angeles: Center for the Study of Evaluation, University of California, 1990.

Pace, C. R. *College Student Experiences Questionnaire: Norms for the Third Edition, 1990.* Los Angeles: Center for the Study of Evaluation, University of California, 1992.

BRENDA JOHNSON-BENSON *is dean of matriculation and counseling at Santa Monica College, Santa Monica, California.*

PETER B. GELTNER *is dean of institutional research at Santa Monica College, Santa Monica, California.*

STEVEN K. STEINBERG *is a professor of English at Los Angeles Southwest College and an adjunct instructor at Santa Monica College.*

This chapter reviews the current literature on support programs tailored to assist the community college transfer student at the four-year institution. The authors discuss useful strategies that may assist administrators and faculty members at four-year colleges and universities in addressing the needs of transfer students through support programs. Support programs, academic performance, and the persistence of transfer students are discussed.

Making the Transition to the Senior Institution

Latrice E. Eggleston, Frankie Santos Laanan

Abundant research has been conducted regarding community college transfer students in conjunction with their academic performance, baccalaureate attainment, and persistence at the four-year college level. A large portion of this research has focused on the *transfer shock* phenomenon, in which transfer students experience a dip in their grade point average during their first or second semester at the four-year institution (Knoell and Medsker, 1965; Cejda and Kaylor, 1997). However, a limited amount of research has been done to study the transfer student's adjustment process, once he or she has reached the senior institution.

Support programs have proven to be an essential element in the success of native students in their academic performance and baccalaureate degree attainment, and such successes are often used as a recruitment tool for various colleges and universities. Support programs tailored toward community college transfer students would have the same effect. A review of the current literature on support programs tailored to assist community college transfer students and literature that deals with the retention, academic performance, and persistence of transfer students provides information to assist administrators and faculty members at four-year colleges and universities in addressing the needs of transfer students through support programs. Understanding the elements that hinder or enhance academic performance, persistence, and graduation rates among transfer students can advance the knowledge currently available regarding the performance and success of community college transfer students at senior institutions.

At least one out of five community college students transfer. Transfer rates vary between 22 and 25 percent nationally among community colleges

NEW DIRECTIONS FOR COMMUNITY COLLEGES, no. 114, Summer 2001 © John Wiley & Sons, Inc.

(Cohen, 1993). Although this number may vary from college to college, it indicates that there exists a market of students whose needs and demands colleges and universities must address. So how do senior institutions develop a means to assist transfer students and help lessen or eliminate the transfer shock these students experience upon entering the university? First, we must understand the needs of these students in order to assess what support programs should provide in an attempt to establish an environment that promotes the opportunity for success and helps reduce the effects of transfer shock.

Characteristics of Transfer Students

Many studies identify the characteristics of transfer students. These students represent various demographics and have various academic histories. Fredrickson (1998) studied over 4,700 students in the University of North Carolina system, who had been enrolled in traditional transfer programs and technical/vocational or occupational programs. Her findings painted an overall picture of the typical transfer student. However, she noted discrepancies in the demographic, school enrollment, employment, and academic persistence patterns.

Transfer students enroll in both traditional and occupational or technical/vocational programs in community colleges and four-year institutions (Frederickson, 1998; Sandeen and Goodale, 1976). Nearly 50 percent of transfer students actually come from technical programs in community colleges. These factors have a direct effect on the preparation of transfer students and their adjustment to senior-level college work, and colleges and universities need to take note of this fact in reaching articulation agreements with community colleges. In addition, community college and university faculty members should become active participants in this process in order to assist students' preparation for senior-level work (Townsend, 1993).

Fredrickson's study (1998) found that, typically, the transfer student was twenty-six years of age, was female, and worked part-time. This picture of the transfer student primarily coincides with national statistic measures. Cohen and Brawer (1996) report from a national survey conducted by the Center for the Study of Community Colleges that the mean age of community college students is twenty-nine, the median is twenty-five, and the mode is nineteen. In Fredrickson's study (1998), however, these statistics vary significantly between students in traditional academic programs and those in technical programs. Although gender does not vary between the two groups of transfer students, the differences in race and age are notable. A larger number of the students on the traditional transfer programs are younger, whereas students in the occupational programs are significantly older.

Fredrickson (1998) notes employment and academic rates to be slightly different for the two groups. Traditional transfer program students are employed more hours than occupational or vocational transfer program students while at the community college, and occupational students graduate in slightly higher numbers than traditional transfer program students. Both groups are academically successful at the university level, but vocational transfer students have slightly higher grades, and traditional transfer program students have slightly higher persistence rates.

Frederickson (1998) found differences in age, gender, and race of students across majors, with students in engineering averaging 26.1 years of age, and students in nursing and undecided majors averaging 28.5 years of age. Students majoring in nursing are 83.3 percent female, whereas only 12.1 percent of the students majoring in engineering are female. Additionally, African American students account for nearly 23 percent of the business students and only 10.6 percent of those in engineering.

Fredrickson's findings (1998) point to several conclusions. Researchers and policymakers who shape support programs must consider the characteristics of the transfer student population in order to address their needs. In particular, while developing support programs, administrators at senior institutions must take into account the demographic makeup, academic backgrounds, enrollment patterns, and academic persistence of community college transfer students.

Another important factor to consider is the ethnicity of potential transfer students. Phillippe and Patton (1999) report for the American Association of Community Colleges that 48 percent of transfer students among first-time freshmen (as of Fall 1997) are racial and ethnic minorities. Ken Carpenter (1991) points out that nearly 75–90 percent of international students who enroll in community colleges intend to transfer. Furthermore, several studies indicate that ethnic minority and international students have particular needs that must be addressed—such as the bridging of language and cultural barriers, academic preparation, and financial aid (Fredrickson, 1998; Rendón and Valadez, 1993). Rendón and Nora (1998) report that Hispanic students typically have very low persistence and retention rates and tend toward poor academic performance in the nation's schools and colleges. They state that there is a need for all educational levels (K–12, community college, and university) to reframe issues and collaborate as one system. They also note that educational reform must make a commitment to a mission, action, budget, and support services for students. In particular, support services must focus on and address the academic, social, and emotional needs of Hispanic students. Therefore, colleges and universities must find a way to address the particular needs of minority students and international students. Transfer students vary in age, gender, race, ethnicity, employment patterns, persistence, academic backgrounds, and socioeconomic backgrounds. Differences in individual characteristics will influence how we address their collective needs through support programs. Universities and their student affairs offices must be ready to receive these students, once they arrive on their campuses.

Needs of Transfer Students at Senior Institutions

Once students reach the university, there are several needs they have that must be addressed if they are going to successfully earn a bachelor's degree. In their monograph (1976), Sandeen and Goodale update and consolidate research problems and the needs of transfer students that continue to exist at colleges and universities. They identify a variety of issues transfer students must deal with, once they reach the university, which include negative attitudes toward transfer students, admissions issues, registration problems, new student programs issues, problems with academic advising, student financial aid problems, housing issues, problems with student activities involvement, career planning and placement issues, publication resources, adjustment to institutional change, articulation, and special academic opportunities.

Sandeen and Goodale's findings (1976) continue to have an impact on current college administrators and personnel at the four-year level. Gardner and Barefoot (1995) note that transfer students commonly face issues involving both academic concerns (academic skills and performance, faculty-student interaction, advising and planning, and career focus) and social concerns (level of self-confidence, campus adjustment and involvement, personal management, and finances). To rectify this situation, admissions officers must make special efforts to assist students in understanding articulation of courses and provide them with the opportunity to have an equal chance in transferring all coursework. New student orientation programs should be developed specifically to help transfer students navigate institutional structures and the campus community. There is a strong need for these programs to be exclusive to transfer students. These orientation programs should not be intertwined with freshman student orientations. Although transfer students encounter similar issues in adjusting to the academic and social milieu of the college or university, their needs are often quite different. Because of issues of course articulation and selection, registration for transfer students is often difficult. In particular, transfer students have a hard time in course selection because many courses are closed before these students actually register, or a particular program is closed to applicants at the junior level. In addition, recent studies indicate that transfer students continue to face many problems with articulation, registration, financial aid, rigorous academic demands, and other challenges, which hinder their persistence to the baccalaureate degree (Laanan, 1996; Townsend, 1995; Cejda, 1994).

Barbara Townsend (1995) conducted a study to identify the possible barriers to the transfer process and the retention efforts for community college students at senior institutions. Through a qualitative approach, she explored several of her beliefs regarding obstacles in the transfer process for community college students. She used a case study method to gather data to support her hypotheses. A sample of fourteen students was obtained from a population of forty students who attended an urban community college and transferred to a private four-year institution. These students had no previous senior-level experience. In-depth interviews and a survey instrument were used to understand the student's transfer process and academic experiences at the community college and the university.

Townsend (1995) discovered several perceptions among students regarding the transfer process. She notes that students commonly reported a "self-reliant" role in the transfer process, as shown in their statements that they neither sought nor received any help from the community college in the transfer process and that they mostly relied on friends and relatives for information. Additionally, they reported that four-year admissions representatives were most helpful. Townsend believes that students took on this self-reliant role because they perceived that institutions failed to communicate with them. Students typically viewed the transfer process as easy, university representatives as more helpful than community college personnel, and themselves as self-reliant.

Students reported their perception that academic standards were said to be higher at the university than at the community college, yet faculty members at the community college were more helpful in the students' academic process. Faculty members at the university were noted as being available outside of class; however, some students viewed university faculty members negatively, in terms of how well they helped them understand course content. Townsend (1995) noted that university faculty members perpetuated a Darwinian attitude of "survival of the fittest" toward community college students.

Student adjustment to senior institutions may also vary according to race, ethnicity, and cultural background. Carpenter (1991) contends that international students often face a particular set of transfer problems in the transfer process that are caused by cultural differences. The lack of knowledge international students have regarding the U.S. educational system, course articulation, and adequate college support acts as a barrier to their baccalaureate degree attainment.

Rendón and Valadez (1993) also contend that there are certain barriers Hispanic students face in the transfer process that hinder their degree attainment at senior institutions. They report that the importance of family, economic considerations, knowledge of the system, cultural understandings, and the relationships of community college administration and faculty with senior-level institutions regarding articulation play a critical role in successful transfer for Hispanic students. College administrators and staff and faculty members must assist in creating a campus environment that eliminates barriers to persistence and that is sensitive to the needs of Hispanic and other minority students.

Thus, in establishing and implementing support services for transfer students, administrators must take into account the needs of transfer students by addressing problems with admissions, registration, orientation, cultural diversity, negative perceptions, academic advising, course articulation, and financial concerns.

Level of Senior Institutions' Response to the Needs of Transfer Students

Support programs specifically for transfer students do not formally exist in most senior institutions, although students continue to experience problems in adjusting to these campus environments. Thus, most of the previous research says that senior institutions are not meeting the needs of transfer students. Furthermore, Townsend's study (1995), as well as those of others, indicates that four-year institutions are showing minimal effort in addressing the needs of transfer students. Current research provides some evidence that a few institutions are attempting to make greater strides in addressing transfer students' needs, whereas others are barely responding. Most recently, Swing (2000) contends that senior institutions are making a minimal attempt to respond to the needs of transfer students through a variety of support programs. These programs include orientation programs, appointed transfer student advocates/liaisons, faculty/staff and peer advising, survival skills courses, special seminars, special housing, and summer institutes or bridge programs. Swing (2000) asserts that "transfer students receive only modest institutional support whether transferring in or out of the [senior] institution"(p. 3).

Swing (2000) reports on the Policy Center on the First Year of College survey, which was conducted to explore what sixty four-year colleges and universities—in Virginia, North Carolina, South Carolina, and Georgia—were doing to meet the needs of transfer students. Through this e-mail-based survey, information was gathered on the existing transfer support programs and services offered by these institutions. Of the thirty-eight institutions that responded, Swing found that nearly a third of the campuses reported that they did not have "special support programs for transfer students," whereas 69 percent of the institutions responded that they had some special support programs for transfer students. These programs ranged from exclusive transfer orientation programs (45 percent) to combined freshman and transfer programs with special sessions for transfer students (21 percent), to a combination of exclusive and inclusive transfer/freshman orientation programs, to extended orientation programs or support programs (28 percent), to assistance with transfer to another institution.

Potential Model Support Programs for Transfer Students

Although there is a limited amount of research on the development and evaluation of support programs, existing programs can serve as an initial starting point for future expansion. In recent years, senior institutions have been shifting to a more responsive attitude toward transfer student needs, as they attempt to increase their efforts to recruit, retain, and graduate transfer students. Thus, some leaders are working to establish and evaluate support programs for transfer students.

In 1985, Vassar College in Poughkeepsie, New York, developed the Exploring Transfer (ET) program, which sought to increase the persistence and matriculation of transfer students from LaGuardia Community College. (Since 1985, the program has included other community colleges.) Initially, twenty-seven students were housed at Vassar College and matriculated into two Vassar courses during the summer (Chenoweth, 1998). Students were able to experience college life and the academic demands of senior college courses.

The success of the ET program was explored in a 1996 report, "Transforming Students' Lives: How 'Exploring Transfer' Works, and Why." Chenoweth (1998) notes that at the time of the report, 255 (64 percent) of the 399 students who participated and completed the program (191 from LaGuardia Community College) transferred to four-year institutions. In addition, of this 64 percent, 97 students earned bachelor's degrees and 33 went on to graduate school, with 21 of these students earning graduate degrees. Vassar College has successfully provided access to transfer for participants in the ET program.

Ackermann (1991) evaluated a similar support program that provided incoming freshman and transfer students with the opportunity to become acquainted with the academic and social environment of the campus through a summer bridge program. She surveyed 265 students who had participated in the Freshman Summer Program (FSP) and Transfers Summer Program (TSP) in Summer 1988 at the University of California, Los Angeles (UCLA). Of those 265 students, 31 responded from the TSP group.

The FSP and TSP programs had several goals. They sought to (1) facilitate student transitions, (2) increase the potential for persistence, retention, and graduation, (3) facilitate the development of critical thinking, academic skills, and personal and social responsibility, (4) introduce Academic Advancement Program retention services (counseling, tutoring, and learning skills), (5) promote appreciation for racial, cultural, and socioeconomic diversity, and (6) build and reinforce a positive self-image, inner confidence, and self-direction among program participants. In general, students have reported that these goals have been reached.

The demographic patterns of the TSP students were diverse. Fifty-two percent of the students were female, 48 percent male, 36 percent Chicano, 36 percent black, 20 percent Latino, and 8 percent Filipino. National trends and patterns of transfer students were also reflected in this study. Fifty-six percent of these students worked part-time, 59 percent also worked off-campus, and 74 percent reported that they spent time every week taking care of family responsibilities, whereas only 37 percent reported that they participated in extracurricular activities.

Ackermann (1991) contrasted the summer grade point averages (GPA) of students with their first- and second-quarter GPA and looked at the influence of their GPA on persistence patterns to the third quarter. TSP students received an average summer GPA of 2.74, fall quarter GPA of 2.21, and spring quarter GPA of 2.32. Although this indicates that TSP students still experienced transfer shock, the summer bridge program indirectly influenced the persistence patterns of students in the program. It should also be noted that these students took at least two courses in the summer and three courses in the fall and in the spring, which may account for a larger gap in GPA from the summer to fall and spring quarters. Among the transfer students, black students earned the highest overall GPA of 2.49, and Chicano, Latino, and Filipino students earned average GPAs of 2.4, 2.26, and 2.1, respectively. The higher GPAs were correlated with the attendance patterns of students in courses. Students who attended class regularly had better grades then those who did not. TSP provided students with the necessary discipline to perform at their higher levels by encouraging and assisting them in making class attendance a necessity and indirectly a "study skill" habit. Ackermann also noted that students' GPAs were a factor in their persistence patterns to the third quarter at UCLA. Ninety-three percent of students went on to enroll in their third quarter at UCLA. Students indicated that the summer bridge program adequately prepared them for the classroom and interaction with others. They were generally satisfied with the availability and quality of services provided, although TSP students underused such campus support services as academic advising, tutoring, professional seminars, psychological counseling, and housing.

Ackermann's findings (1991) and her study of the summer bridge program can be a guide for future programs that seek to establish support for transfer students and whose goals are to increase the retention, persistence, and graduation rates of transfer students at senior institutions.

Another potential program model can be taken from the University of Arkansas and its Office for Non-Traditional Students (ONTS). This program caters to the needs of nontraditional transfer students—both prospective and currently enrolled. ONTS works "to provide prospective and currently enrolled non-traditional students with support, services, information, and resources to meet their unique needs, and to enhance their opportunity for success at the University of Arkansas" (University of Arkansas, 1999). In addition, ONTS provides nontraditional transfer students with assistance in child care, housing, employment, adjustment to the University campus, tutoring resources, study skills, mentoring, and peer counseling.

The University of Illinois at Urbana-Champaign has also recently developed a program to provide academic, personal, and financial support to transfer students. The Multicultural Transfer Admissions Program (MTAP) seeks to provide counseling for prospective transfer students through open houses, advising sessions, course articulation resources through the Internet, and campus visits and tours. The program works to service students once they reach the campus as well. In order to retain newly recruited students on campus and assist in their transition to the campus community, students are given a graduate student adviser, who provides direction to campus resources, conducts various workshops in such areas as study skills, internship, and résumé writing, and organizes welcome receptions for transfer students.

Of the four support programs described in this chapter, Vassar's ET program and Ackermann's summer bridge program (1991) are the only examples of a support program that has proven to be valuable and successful in the retention, persistence, and graduation rates of transfer students. Although these programs do not look at comparative measures of transfer students who use or do not use its services with respect to the effects of transfer shock, what we do know about their success in the persistence and retention areas is quite remarkable and should be noted for the future development of programs to address the transfer shock phenomenon. There is no research currently available to assess the success or failure of the ONTS program, so we are unable to make any conclusions regarding its efforts. Because the University of Illinois's MTAP program is fairly new and is continuously evolving over time, time will be a factor in the evaluation of its program model's success as well.

Conclusion

Transfer students are a very diverse group of students; they vary in age, gender, racial and ethnic background, academic preparation, and employment patterns—among other things. Transfer students report a need for more course articulation, counseling and advising, faculty sensitivity, academic support services, transfer student-centered orientation programs, student activities, and knowledge of campus resources, and universities and colleges are not meeting their needs. Senior institutions are only just beginning to develop programs especially for transfer students. There is a strong need for senior institutions to continue to develop support programs for transfer students to enhance their retention and persistence.

There is a need for further research in the area of program development and evaluation for support programs that assist the transition of transfer students at four-year universities and colleges. Policy implementations that enhance the academic performance, social growth, and persistence patterns of transfer students are imperative for success in the development and implementation of support programs for transfer students. Once programs are established, we can evaluate their effectiveness in reducing or eliminating the transfer shock experienced by transfer students. A demonstrated commitment by higher education to address this issue is ultimately needed.

References

Ackermann, S. P. "The Benefits of Summer Bridge Programs for Underrepresented and Low-Income Transfer Students." *Community/Junior College Quarterly of Research and Practice,* 1991, *15,* 211–224.

Carpenter, K. "Serving the Transfer Needs of International Students: Cooperation Between Two-Year and Four-Year Schools." *College and University,* 1991, *6*(3), 63–66.

Cejda, B. D. "Reducing Transfer Shock Through Faculty Collaboration: A Case Study." *Community College Journal of Research and Practice,* 1994, *18,* 189–199.

Cejda, B. D., and Kaylor, A. J. "Academic Performance of Community College Transfer Students at Private and Liberal Arts Colleges." *Community College Journal of Research and Practice,* 1997, *21,* 651–659.

Chenoweth, K. "The New Faces of Vassar: This Seven Sister College Has Tapped into an Often Overlooked Resource of Minority Undergraduates—Transfer Students." *Black Issues in Higher Education,* 1998, *14*(26), 22–23.

Cohen, A. "Analyzing Community College Student Transfer Rates." Paper presented at the annual meeting of the American Educational Research Association, Atlanta, Apr. 1993.

Cohen, A. M., and Brawer, F. B. *The American Community College.* (3rd ed.) San Francisco: Jossey-Bass, 1996.

Fredrickson, J. "Today's Transfer Students: Who Are They?" *Community College Review,* 1998, *26*(1), 43–45.

Knoell, D. M., and Medsker, L. L. *From Junior to Senior College: A National Study of the Transfer Student.* Washington, D.C.: American Council of Education, 1965.

Laanan, F. S. "Making the Transition: Understanding the Adjustment Process of Community College Transfer Students." *Community College Review,* 1996, *23*(4), 69–84.

Phillippe, K., and Patton, M. *National Profile of Community Colleges: Trends and Statistics.* (3rd ed.) Washington, D.C.: Community College Press, American Association of Community Colleges, 1999.

Rendón, L. I., and Nora, A. "Hispanic Students: Stopping the Leaks in the Pipeline." *Educational Record,* 1998, *69*(1), 79–85.

Rendón, L. I., and Valadez, J. R. "Qualitative Indicators of Hispanic Student Transfer." *Community College Review,* 1993, *20*(4), 27–37.

Sandeen, A., and Goodale, T. *The Transfer Student: An Action Agenda for Higher Education.* Gainesville: Institute of Higher Education, University of Florida, 1976. (ED 154 750)

Swing, R. L. *Transfer Student Support Programs.* Brevard, N.C.: Policy Center on the First Year of College, Brevard College, 2000.

Townsend, B. K. "University Practices That Hinder the Academic Success of Community College Transfer Students." Paper presented at the 18th annual meeting of the Association for the Study of Higher Education, Pittsburgh, Pa., 1993. (ED 363 360)

Townsend, B. K. "Community College Transfer Students: A Case Study of Survival." *Review of Higher Education,* 1995, *18,* 175–193.

"University of Arkansas, Office for Non-Traditional Students." [http://www. uark.edu /admin/onts]. Dec. 1999.

LATRICE E. EGGLESTON is a doctoral student in the Department of Educational Policy Studies at the University of Illinois at Urbana-Champaign.

FRANKIE SANTOS LAANAN is assistant professor of community college leadership in the Department of Human Resource Education at the University of Illinois at Urbana-Champaign.

The authors discuss the role of the community college in preparing students to transfer to a four-year postsecondary institution. Issues about institutional support, quality of education, and academic rigor are discussed, as well as how institutions can implement innovative approaches to the transfer function.

9

Leadership Perspectives on Preparing Transfer Students

Phoebe K. Helm, Arthur M. Cohen

This chapter presents two perspectives on preparing transfer students: first, a presidential perspective on preparing and facilitating the movement of students from community colleges to four-year institutions, and second, a discussion about the extent to which community colleges might improve their transfer rates.

A Presidential Perspective

What can presidents of community colleges do to support transfer? All would agree that the quality of the faculty, the reputation of the college, and strong articulation agreements are key factors in transfer success. But to increase the number of transfers, presidents need to set clear expectations, invest in research, examine policy and practice, build relationships and programs, and provide visibility.

Presidents can set the agenda for their colleges, and in doing so, they can raise expectations for transfer. These expectations need to permeate the advising and admissions processes and faculty roles. It must be clear that it is not enough to assist only students who enter with a declared intent to transfer. Community colleges must expand the horizons for students who may not know that a four-year degree is a reasonable goal for them to consider.

If presidents have transfer as a priority, then they must support research to measure progress toward that goal and identify ways to improve it. In examining who transfers and who does not, including both demographic and programmatic factors, much can be learned to guide colleges in making change. In addition, a search of the literature can identify programs to be replicated.

Community colleges should review their own policies and practices to see if they aggressively support transfer. Are students advised in a manner that enables them to transfer 60–64 credit hours within a period of two years, including summers, or have colleges accepted 12 credit hours as full-time as defined by financial aid? Are students shown the impact on their earnings by completing their degrees faster? Clearly, there is nothing inherently wrong with being a part-time student, but there is reason for concern if the alternatives are not overtly made available to students.

Colleges need to be more aggressive in helping students limit the number of courses that transfer as electives and to focus on courses that meet general education or program requirements. Similarly, students in career programs, which provide options in mathematics and science, should be encouraged to strongly consider the transfer courses. In addition, colleges need to compare the credit hour value of courses with that of the same courses at the universities to which their students transfer.

Effective Transfer Programs and Linkages

Presidents can help their colleges build relationships with universities by developing relationships with their presidents and by supporting faculty relationships and providing incentives for faculty members to work together on grants and other programs of mutual interest. One example of the outcome of such efforts is the Truman College/DePaul University Bridge Program. This program recognizes that transitions from one institution to another are not always smooth for many students, because they are moving into unfamiliar territory. To facilitate student transition, teams of faculty members identify courses that should be taken by sophomores. Selected faculty members at each institution team-teach these courses. Students from each institution are enrolled in the course, which meets at Truman for the first half of the term and at DePaul for the second half. A faculty member of the university is housed at Truman and serves as an adviser for students at both institutions. This program, now in its fourth year, has successfully transitioned more than two hundred students and is supported by a grant.

Other programs that work include a scholars program at Triton College, which is designed to prepare students for very competitive universities. Other colleges and universities have implemented dual admissions programs in which the student is admitted to the community college and the university simultaneously. As long as the student follows the prescribed program, junior status at the university and the transfer of credits are assured. First-generation, low-income and/or minority students often need more assistance to persist and to transfer. Transfer clubs could develop cohort support groups to visit universities, pursue scholarships, and use faculty advisers to support and guide their decisions and to stay in touch with them after they transfer.

Finally, presidents can give visibility to their transfer programs, students, and faculty members. Given that community college students who transfer generally do as well as students who began at the university, why do we not see advertisement to that effect? Our students are success stories. If these data were systematically gathered and shared with these students' high schools, the universities, and the media, would not the number of transfers increase?

Institutional Role in Improving the Transfer Rate

A volume concerning transfer students, their successes, the obstacles they face, and the various influences affecting their progress should include a note about policies and practices that institutions adopt to make transfer retain its place as a central community college function. From the beginnings of community colleges more than one hundred years ago, transfer has been at the heart of the institutions. The colleges began as feeders from high school to university and, despite the popularity of occupational studies and various forms of community service, they have never relinquished that role. More than half their curriculum consists of courses in the liberal arts similar to those offered at four-year colleges and universities. More than 20 percent of their students transfer each year to in-state public universities, a figure that has not deviated for more than a decade. The colleges are integral to America's postsecondary effort. Yet, as with most aspects of education, we can do better. What can institutions do to ensure that there are few obstacles on students' paths from high school to the upper division of universities? The lower schools have been accused of not preparing students well enough and the universities are charged with being aloof and unreceptive. But here we speak of the community colleges themselves, where transfer rates vary widely between states and between colleges in the same state. What can they do?

A step toward or away from transfer is part of the history of each college. Students, their parents, high school faculty members and counselors, the local news media—all have a view of their college that sees it as more or less favorable toward moving students through toward the baccalaureate degree. These perceptions are difficult to change; they relate to transfer rates that have prevailed for many years. A college in one community may be perceived as an economical first choice for well-prepared students who intend eventually to transfer, whereas a college in a similar community may be known as the place that students should avoid if they expect ever to receive bachelor's degrees. Changing these perceptions is a long-term process and those who seek to do so should not expect rapid progress.

How might these perceptions be changed? The idea of transfer begins in the president's office. If a president is determined to modify the community's view of the college as an environment favorable to transfer, many things can be done. First, of course, valid data on the institution's transfer rate should be maintained. These data should be collected consistently according to readily understandable definitions, and they should be presented straightforwardly so that the public is not confused by all sorts of permutations. In other words, the college publicizes a figure based on the percentage of students who begin at the institution with no prior college experience, complete at least four courses there, and matriculate at an in-state university within a specified period of time, say four or five years. If the college transfers a high proportion of its students to a nearby out-of-state institution, which is often the case when a college is in a border community, those data can be part of the presentation. The data may show that the college's transfer rate is higher or lower than the state average. The data should not be clouded with subsets of the number of various population groups or students who did or did not indicate a desire to transfer when they entered. The important point is that the public should receive data collected in a consistent fashion year after year so that they trust what they see.

Different strategies need to be pursued in colleges with high or low transfer rates. Where the rate is high, the intention is to sustain or build on that success. Here, the major effort should be put on ensuring that articulation of courses and programs with the local university is kept current. Each college has only a small number of universities to which most of its transferring students go. And within those universities are only a small number of programs into which most of its transfers matriculate. Thus, articulation agreements showing how many and what types of courses are acceptable must be kept current. There should be no excuse for a student's having trouble in transferring credit to a university where sizable proportions of that college's transfers go. And each of the most popular programs—usually business, psychology, or some health or technical field—should have courses closely connected so that the college provides the prerequisites readily accepted by the faculty in the students' major of choice. Within the college, these articulation agreements are well publicized through a transfer center or some other administrative agency so that accurate information is available. The choice of courses or the recommendations for prerequisites cannot be left to information contributed by the faculty or staff members who, however well-meaning, may not have the most current requirements to report.

The college with a high transfer rate will likely have an honors program that is useful in recruiting the best students from the local high schools. It will have a routine pattern of recognizing students who transfer, reporting their names, the institutions where they are going, and the majors that they are entering. The college will also have staff members who articulate financial aid with their counterparts at the receiving universities so that students do not have to begin the process all over again in an unfamiliar environment.

The college with a low transfer rate must approach things differently. Low transfer rates begin with the types of students the college attracts. If the local high school teachers and counselors advise their better students to go elsewhere, the college staff has its work cut out. The high school staff must be nurtured through frequent visits from college faculty and staff members. Faculty members should meet with their counterparts in the local high school and consider how their courses are similar or different, as well as what course requirements, types of tests, and textbooks make the college courses a natural succession. The high school students should be invited to attend classes at the college so that they can see the feasibility of entering classes that will be familiar to them. The college should sponsor high school "days," occasions when sizable numbers of students from single local schools are brought to the campus, shown around, treated to lunch, and otherwise made to feel welcome. In other words, the idea that the college is the place to start one's postsecondary experience has to be successfully communicated to the best students in the local feeder high schools.

At the college where the transfer rate is low, the data should be publicized nonetheless. It can take several years before the transfer rate is affected, but the college that starts from a transfer rate of 5 or 6 percent and adds 1 percentage point to that rate records a significant increase. The college can increase the rate only by attracting its share of baccalaureate-bound students. And because it takes only a few transferring students to effect a notable increase, a few unrestricted scholarships can make a big difference. Getting the university to guarantee admission for these few students completes the picture.

To sum up, if increasing a college's transfer rate is seen as desirable, then different strategies should be followed, depending on the current rate. For the colleges with high transfer rates, maintaining current information on programs and financial aid in the universities and majors to which most of their students transfer is essential. In the colleges with low transfer rates, changing the public's perception of the college as a desirable place to start postsecondary study is the first priority. No number of articulation agreements with universities will be of any value if the local high school staff members and the students and their parents see the college as the wrong place to start if the student is serious about progress toward the baccalaureate.

PHOEBE K. HELM is president of Harry S. Truman College, one of the City Colleges of Chicago.

ARTHUR M. COHEN is professor of higher education in the Graduate School of Education and Information Studies at UCLA and director of the ERIC Clearinghouse for Community Colleges.

INDEX

"Academic alliances" model (UCLA), 36–37
Ackerman, S.P., 64, 93, 94, 95
Adams, J., 63
Adelman, C., 49, 54, 63, 66
Adjustment, transfer, 8–10
African American Scholars Program (AASP), 19
African American students: performance assessment of, 42; transfer rates of, 15–16, 17. *See also* Minority transfer students
African American Transfer Center, 19
Alexander, H., 62
Allard, S., 65
Alpha Gamma Sigma, 37
American Association of Community and Junior Colleges, 26
American Association of Community Colleges, 89
Andrew, L. D., 9
Anglin, L. W., 65
Archer, E., 16
Armstrong, W. B., 66
Arnold, C. L., 62, 63, 65
Arnold, J. C., 2, 45, 46, 59
ASSIST (Articulation System Stimulating Interinstitutional Student Transfer), 18
Astin, A. W., 10, 79
Austin, C. G., 32, 33

Bach, S. K., 57
Baker, R. W., 79
Banks, D. L., 36, 37
Barefoot, 90
Barr, J. E., 62, 66
Bean, J. P., 9
Bean and Metzner Attrition Model, 9
Beginning Postsecondary Student Longitudinal Study (BPS), 6, 63
Bender, L. W., 15, 17, 19
Bennett, C., 9
Bentley-Baker, K., 26
Bers, T. H., 64
Big Bend Community College (BBCC), 68–69
Blau, J. R., 62
Boughan, K., 62, 63, 64, 65

Brantley, F., 62, 65
Brawer, F. B., 1, 5, 7, 8, 17, 66, 68, 88
Brint, S., 15, 19
"Build Your Own Honors Program" workshop (UCLA), 31, 36
Bunn, C. E., 16, 65
Burns, D., 42
Byock, G., 36, 37
Byxbe, F. R., 63, 64, 65

California AB 1725 legislation, 17–18
California Articulation Number System (CANS) course sequencing, 18
California Community Colleges, 21
California Community Colleges Chancellor's Office (CCCCO), 80
California Senate Bill 121, 18
California State University (CSU), 77
California State University systems, 18, 26
Camden County College, 70
Campus climate, 10–11
Carlan, P. E., 63, 64, 65
Carpenter, K., 89, 91
Carroll, C. D., 6, 15, 19, 63
Carter, D. F., 9, 10
Case, L. B., 21
Casey, K. L., 65
Cathey, S. A., 66
CCWD (Department of Community Colleges and Workforce Development, Oregon), 46, 59. *See also* OUS/CCWD project study
Cejda, B. D., 22, 62, 65, 69, 87, 90
Center for Academic Interinstitutional Programs (CAIP), 28
Center for the Study of Community Colleges, 88
Chenoweth, K., 93
Chickering, A. W., 10
City College Honors Student Council (San Diego), 37
City College of San Francisco, 65
Clemons, J., 28
Cohen, A. M., 1, 2, 5, 7, 8, 15, 17, 66, 68, 88, 99
College adjustment: campus climate and, 10–11; comparisons of transfer/native student, 8; educational environment

ment role of, 26; founding of, 25; resolving elitism issues of, 33
San Francisco State University, 21
Sanchez, J. R., 66
Sandeen, A., 88, 90
Santa Ana College, 20
Santa Monica College (SMC), 77
Santa Monica College project: background of, 78; implications for practice from results of, 84; ongoing research of, 82–84; origins of, 77–78; overview of, 78–82; Santa Monica College Transfer Students' Questionnaire used in, 79–82, 81t, 83t; Santa Monica College/UCLA student involvement in, 78–79; UCLA Transfer Students' Questionnaire used in, 79–82
Santa Monica College Transfer Students' Questionnaire (SMC-TSQ), 79–82, 81t, 83t
Saupe, J. L., 62
"Scholars program," 32
Senior institutions: level of response to transfer students by, 92; needs of transfer students at, 90–92; potential model support programs at, 93–95
Shaffer, B., 64, 65
Shelby State Community College, 19
Sheldon, M. S., 17
Shymoniak, L., 62
Sigworth, D., 66
Siryk, B., 79
Skinner, E. F., 15
Smart, J., 8
Smedley, B. D., 10
Snowden, M., 65
Spicer, S. L., 66
Spuler, A., 9, 10
Standing Committee on Honors in the Two-Year College (National Collegiate Honors Council), 26
Steinberg, S. K., 2, 77
Stewart, D. M., 15, 16
Student performance: assessing minority, 42; OUS/CCWD project study on student transfers and, 49–52t, 57–59; transfer shock and decline in, 5–6, 7–8, 57–59. See also GPAs
Students. See Transfer students
SUCCESS Project (San Diego Community College District), 32, 34
Summer Scholars Transfer Institute (SSTI), 20, 22

Swing, R. L., 92
Sworder, S., 64

A Tale of Two Cities (Dickens), 39
Thornton, J. W., Jr., 7
Timmons, F. R., 66
Tinto, V., 8, 10
Tobolowsky, B., 17
Townsend, B. K., 5, 22, 65, 66, 68, 88, 90, 91, 92
Transfer adjustment process, 8–9
Transfer Alliance Program (TAP), 26, 28–31, 36
Transfer barriers: described, 15–17; policy and programmatic changes to address, 17–19; successful programs addressing, 19–21; transfer center to address, 17
Transfer Behavior Among Beginning Postsecondary Students: 1989-94 (McCormick and Carroll), 6
Transfer centers, 17
Transfer credits, 17
Transfer Day Fairs (Glendale Community College), 21
Transfer Education Advisory Committee (Santa Monica College), 82
Transfer programs: articulation agreements governing, 40–41; facilitating minority student transfers, 41–42; importance of, 87; leadership for effective, 100–101; transfer centers, 17; university-devised incentive, 27
Transfer rates: of community colleges, 15, 87–88; institutional role in improving, 100–103; racial/ethnic differences in, 15–16, 17, 89–90; recommendations for enhancing, 22
Transfer shock: GPA decline due to, 5–6, 7–8; OUS/CCWD project study on, 55, 57–58; research focused on, 87; studies on, 65–66
Transfer student studies: making use of the data in, 70–71; methods used in, 63–65; models of, 67–70; researchers of, 62–63; Santa Monica College project, 77–84
Transfer students: adjustment process of, 8–11; personal, demographic, and environmental characteristics associated with, 8–9, 88–90; presidential perspective on preparing, 99–100; reports on transfer behavior of, 6–7; response level of senior institutions to, 92; senior institutions and needs of,

Back Issue/Subscription Order Form

Copy or detach and send to:
Jossey-Bass, 350 Sansome Street, San Francisco CA 94104-1342

Call or fax toll free!
Phone 888-378-2537 6AM-5PM PST; Fax 800-605-2665

Back issues: Please send me the following issues at $28 each
(Important: please include series initials and issue number, such as CC90)

1. CC _____

_____

$ _____ Total for single issues

$ _____ Shipping charges (for single issues *only;* subscriptions are exempt
from shipping charges): Up to $30, add $5^{50} • $30^{01}–$50, add $6^{50}
$50^{01}–$75, add $8 • $75^{01}–$100, add $10 • $100^{01}–$150, add $12
Over $150, call for shipping charge

Subscriptions   Please ❏ start ❏ renew my subscription to *New Directions
for Community Colleges* for the year ___ at the following rate:

U.S.:	❏ Individual $63	❏ Institutional $115
Canada:	❏ Individual $63	❏ Institutional $155
All Others:	❏ Individual $87	❏ Institutional $189

NOTE: Subscriptions are quarterly, and are for the calendar year only.
Subscriptions begin with the Spring issue of the year indicated above.

$ _____ Total single issues and subscriptions (Add appropriate sales tax for
your state for single issue orders. No sales tax for U.S. subscriptions.
Canadian residents, add GST for subscriptions and single issues.)

❏ Payment enclosed (U.S. check or money order only)

❏ VISA, MC, AmEx, Discover Card #_____ Exp. date_____

Signature _____ Day phone _____

❏ Bill me (U.S. institutional orders only. Purchase order required)

Purchase order #_____

Federal Tax ID 13559 3032   GST 89102-8052

Name _____

Address _____

_____

Phone_____ E-mail _____

For more information about Jossey-Bass, visit our Web site at:
www.josseybass.com   **PRIORITY CODE = ND1**